HEARTS ON FIRE!

Your Roadmap To
An Exciting, Love-Filled Life

ROBERT SAMUEL KING

DEDICATION PAGE

- To my beloved and loving God: Father, Son and Holy Spirit
- To my parents – true disciples of Jesus
- To my Aunt Sandra – a disciple set on fire with God's love
- To the churches that nurtured me in my Christian faith – Clark Memorial, Stones River, Brentwood, Crestwood, the campus ministry and Chapel at Clark Atlanta University, Central and Emory
- To the wonderful colleagues of mine – pastors with hearts aflame
- To the flock that I currently serve
- And for younger, coming generations of Jesus followers who will live with their hearts set on fire with Jesus's love all around the world

CONTENTS

Section 1: Introduction

Section II: Lighting the Fire:
How Our Hearts Burn Bright with Excitement,
Purpose and Christlike Love

Section III: Spreading the Fire: Changing the World by Loving Our Neighbors

Section IV: Epilogue

SECTION 1

Introduction

CHAPTER 1

Prologue:
Seeking and Finding the
Way Home

Greetings, Buenos Dias, أهلا و سهلا,
Annyeonghaseyo, שלום,
and O Si'Yo Wonderful Person!

Have you ever been lost before? Whether it was following Google Maps or Waze to see friends or family, playing hide-and-go-seek in a big pasture in the country, or traveling on an international trip for business or pleasure, we have all had a moment where we look up and realize we are not where we need to be! When you get lost like that as a child, that moment feels like life or death, like you'll never get home.

I felt like that once when I was about 10 years old. I was playing in my dad's office in Nashville, TN where he worked. He and his co-workers had gone to a meeting, and he had left me to my toys and play while they met in another area on the campus. He wasn't too far away, but while he was away, something frightening happened: the security alarm started going off. And I was afraid! I was lost and separated from my Dad who loved me, and I didn't know what to do.

I started calling for my Daddy; the alarm was blazing, the flashing red light sending shockwaves of fear through my body. Even though I knew the office where I was, I didn't know where he was. He would come find me, wouldn't he? What was I going to do?

After what felt like forever, he and his coworkers finally returned. He scooped me up and hugged me and comforted me in my crying. I felt the warmth of his love and my heart was comforted, warm again with life and hope.

That's a story about my experience being lost as a child, but here's why I shared that with you, Wonderful Person:

All of us can experience moments in life where we feel lost, separated from true life: a life burning brightly with purpose, passion, true happiness and love. We search for the love of the One who loves us, but we often don't know where to find that love. We search for the security and the warmth of being embraced with such a love that has the power to heal our hearts, change our lives and empower us to change the world. But like helpless children crying out in the darkness, we don't know where to turn. We seek a life of excitement and direction, but we often don't know where to look.

Our communities, our institutions, our churches, and our world is desperately crying out, seeking to find such a life and such a love. But sadly, we either don't know our way home or we are misled. We can be misled by those who don't love us, those who deceive us to walk a path that doesn't bring us home, home to the heart of the One who loves us.

People from all generations and cultures are crying out for more in this life than the lost paths we find in today's world. The spiritual alarm is sounding about these lost ways: the lost ways of empty relationships and life without divine direction, the lost ways of having full bank accounts yet living in spiritual poverty, the lost ways of abundant connection with technology but few authentic relationships with close friends, family and others in life.

At this tipping point in the life of the world, this cry for home has pierced my soul for far too long. This book is my response to that cry – that search for true life and a healthy home.

In the biblical book of Proverbs, King Solomon writes that the human heart is the wellspring from which everything in life flows. (Proverbs 4:23) Wonderful Person, our hearts are the spiritual containers in which the love, peace, purpose and excitement that God created us for are designed to live.

I am writing this book as a roadmap for all of the human family to come home to that exact spiritual wellspring of love, purpose, excitement and direction. I am writing this book as a roadmap home into the warm embrace of Jesus's love so that our hearts can burn with wonderfully new life, purpose, excitement and love. I believe with all my heart that this book can guide you, your loved ones and the entire human family into life with hearts on fire!

This is how I define someone whose heart is set on fire: **their heart burns with the love of Jesus Christ, igniting their life with divine direction, life-changing love of God, self and others, and joyful excitement that sparks change and impacts the world!**

This book is your roadmap to find your way home. This book is your roadmap to come home to a love that will never leave you and a life that will grow in excitement and purpose from day to day. This is the road to a heart on fire! If you are ready to start the journey home, turn to the next page!

CHAPTER 2

Setting the Candle: Preparing Our Hearts For An Exciting Life and Love

I – do – not – like – thunderstorms. Why, you may ask? Beyond the lightning and thunder, I hate when the power goes out. Have you ever been home when your power has gone out at nighttime? It is a frustrating experience, right? You cannot use your microwave, charge your favorite phone or device or use any other appliance. If that wasn't enough, you cannot see! Thanks be to God for candles, those simple small gifts that can make a world of difference when you are walking in the dark. Candles not only provide light, but they also provide heat when they are lit. But to make sure a candle stays lit, you have to make sure that the wick is prepared: up and ready to be set ablaze by a warm and consuming fire.

Just like a candle has to be positioned so it can be lit by a physical fire, so it is spiritually with our hearts and lives. In order for us to live with hearts on fire with divine direction, unconditional love and joyful excitement in Jesus Christ, we have to position our hearts and lives as spiritual candles: ready to be set on fire with the holy love of Christ!

In the Gospels, Jesus outlines how we position ourselves to get ready for the wonderfully exciting flame of His love to consume our hearts and empower us to change the world.

On an ancient Mediterranean mountain in Galilee, Jesus outlines four key ways that we position our hearts like candles awaiting a warm fire. His teaching demonstrates some essential practices of how we prepare ourselves to be set on fire with His wonderful love and direction, in our lives, our families, our communities, our churches, institutions and throughout the entire world. Here are those four keys:

1. **Humility in prayer**
2. **A real encounter with the risen Jesus**
3. **An expectation of the exciting power of the Holy Spirit**
4. **A heart that receives the Holy Spirit with warm worship and gratitude**

Read on if you are ready to feel the exciting fire of His love!

Posture 1: Humility In Prayer

Whether it is on the phone, Zoom or in person, I love a good conversation with a beloved friend, family member or a member from my community of faith. Good conversations with loved ones are life-giving, aren't they? Just like we have our conversations with our physical companions, so Jesus teaches us about another level of conversation: prayer, our ongoing conversation with God.

Jesus helps us to understand. On that mountain in Galilee, Jesus taught his first followers how to pray. This model for prayer has served as the model prayer for every follower of Jesus since then, and it is the same prayer for everyone who wants to be set on fire with His love, direction and excitement today. If we want to position our hearts to burn with love, excitement and direction, we must begin with humility in prayer.

Jesus said: "When you pray, pray in this way, Our Father, who art in heaven, hallowed be thy name, Thy Kingdom come, thy will be done, on earth as it is in heaven. Give us this day our daily bread, and forgive us our trespasses, as we forgive those who trespass against us. Lead us not into temptation but deliver us from the evil one." (Matthew 6:9-13)

In this prayer, Jesus teaches us to pray, "Our Father, hallowed be thy name". Here is the heart of humbling ourselves to experience hearts on set fire through prayer. Humility begins with acknowledging that God is our spiritual parent. When we do, our response is happy praise and adoration: worshipping God in the beauty of God's holiness. (Psalm 29:2) But then as we humble ourselves before God, we offer ourselves as instruments for God's kingdom to come in us and through us.

So, in order for us to experience excitement, true happiness, divine direction and wonderful love from Jesus, we have to first acknowledge our need for God. In order for the hearts of our lives, our families, and our institutions to burn bright with His love, we have to humble ourselves. As we do, God's kingdom of love, joy, peace, patience, kindness, gentleness, generosity, faithfulness, self-control, justice and mercy will come in our lives and through us into the world! (Galatians 5:22-23)

When we humble ourselves, we become ripe for the divine fire of the love of Christ! Let's get ready!

Heart Check Wrap-up

Key Point: Humility through prayer is our first step of preparation to live with hearts on fire.

Thoughts and Questions for Reflection:
- In what areas of your life are you seeking divine direction, guidance and love? In what areas of your family, community or Christian community are you seeking direction, guidance and love?
- Have you ever spent time in prayer with God?
- If so, have you ever prayed the Lord's Prayer?

Posture 2: A Real Encounter with the Living Jesus

Have you ever passed someone by while you are walking or driving down a road? During my many travels in the US and abroad in Europe, Egypt, Morocco, and the Caribbean, I have found that you never quite know who you might encounter when you meet a stranger on a road.

Scripture shows us in the Gospel that sometimes we might just encounter a holy stranger on the road and be forever changed!

Long ago, there were once two friends, who were walking down a Mediterranean road. They were walking with their faces low and to the ground because something tragic had just happened – and they did not know how they would go on afterwards.

Jesus Christ of Nazareth, the Son of the Living God, had come from heaven to earth in their lifetime. Once he began his ministry in adulthood, after three years of healing the sick, raising the dead, forgiving sinners and breaking bread with them, cleansing lepers and proclaiming the kingdom of God was at hand, He was crucified on a Roman Cross, dying a painful, humiliating death. He literally poured out His life to forgive the sins of all who were lost in the world. He gave himself so humanity could come back home to God. And these two friends were followers of this crucified Jesus.

Luke records they had hoped He would redeem Israel and bring the kingdom of God to its fullness (Luke 24:21). But as they walked on that dusty road, their heads were hanging low, and so was their hope.

Until a stranger comes alongside them and starts talking with them. For some reason, this stranger has no idea what has happened with Jesus of Nazareth. Until he begins breaking it all down for them.

He corrects them and begins to unpack the Holy Scriptures, helping them to see what they had missed: Jesus was alive! After they came to their ultimate destination in Emmaus, this holy stranger broke bread with them, gave thanks to God, and gave this bread to the disciples – and they realized that their holy stranger was the risen Jesus Christ!

Then they replied "Were not our hearts *burning* while we were on the road?" (Luke 24:32) When they went back and told the disciples, the Apostles of the Early Church, that Jesus was alive, their hearts were set on fire with hope! When the others found out He was alive, more hearts were set on fire with refreshed hope. The Jesus movement was alive – the best was yet to come!

The risen Jesus meets the disciples on the road from despair to hope. Here's the Good News for us, Wonderful Person: He still meets us today.

Even at this tipping point in the history of the world, the Resurrected Jesus meets us where we are in our pain, brokenness and despair. Thankfully, He also guides us into the hopeful future into which God is leading us.

The second posture which Jesus shows us to prepare our hearts to burn bright with divine direction, joyful excitement and unconditional love is a real encounter *with the Risen Jesus.* More than coming to a building, service or event, this is a life-changing moment He desires for all of us to have as we receive Him. He longs for us to receive Him as He is: Lord, Savior, Risen and Alive. When we receive the Risen Jesus, He will fill our hearts with love for Him, love for ourselves and love for all.

Heart Check Wrap-up

Key Point: A real encounter with the Risen Jesus is our second step of preparation to experience living with hearts on fire.

Thoughts and Questions for Reflection:
- No matter who you are, Jesus Christ is walking with you right where you are in life. How does that make you feel? Comforted? Assured? Curious? Other emotions?
- Can you point to a time where you have experienced the presence of Jesus in a powerful way? If you have not, lift your hands up with your palms open and cry out, "Lord Jesus, I am ready to experience you. I am ready to see you, In your name I pray. Amen."
- If you are part of a Christian community, what ministries currently or in the future could help your community experience the presence of Christ in a new way?

- If you are not yet part of a Christian community, what type of spiritual practices would you value in such a community of faith?

Posture 3: An expectation of the exciting power of the Holy Spirit

Have you ever had to grieve the loss of someone you love? Maybe it was a friend, family member, spouse or someone from your community? I can remember when each of my grandparents passed. Saying goodbye to one you love never is easy.

Scripture helps us to understand when Jesus was saying goodbye to His first friends. In the Gospel of Luke, Luke records that after His Resurrection, Jesus spent 40 days with these disciples, teaching and preparing them for what was next in the movement. (Acts 1:3)

During this season, Jesus spent time pouring out grace when the disciples felt like failures for deserting Him. He spent time clarifying and providing assurance that He was in another level of glory in His resurrected body. He spent time speaking peace into them and giving them the power to forgive sins in His name. He spent time showering them with grace in the midst of their unbelief and amazement at the Resurrection. He ate with them at the seashore, feeding them fish and bread. But He wasn't planning to stay with them in the flesh forever.

During the time Jesus spent with them in Galilee, He also made the disciples a promise. The coming of that promise would give birth to the Church of Jesus Christ and change the world.

He said: "You will receive power when the Holy Spirit has come upon you, and you will be my witnesses, in Jerusalem, in Judea, in Samaria and unto the end of the age." (Acts 1:8) Then the Bible declares that immediately after He said this, he was taken up from them and lifted out of their sight. (Acts 1:9)

They couldn't believe it! How could Jesus come back to them and then leave? But angels told them as they stared into the heavens above:

> "Why do you stand looking toward heaven? This Jesus whom you saw leave you will come again."
>
> (Acts 1:10)

Something big was about to drop, and because of this coming holy explosion, the world would never be the same.

During this last episode in His resurrected body on earth, Jesus reveals the third step of preparation we must take to burn with hearts on fire: an expectation of the exciting power of the Holy Spirit to come and move among our lives!

Heart Check Wrap-up

Key Point: An expectation of the exciting power of the Holy Spirit is the third step of preparation to burn afresh with the divine direction, love and excitement of Jesus.

Thoughts and Questions for Reflection:
- What hopes and promises are you looking forward to happening in your life?
- What promises have you seen God fulfill in your life?
- What areas of your life, your family, your church and/or your city would be blessed by a fresh outpouring of the Holy Spirit?

Posture 4: A heart that receives the Holy Spirit with warm worship and gratitude

Have you ever seen an infant child before? Whether we are parents, grandparents, aunts, uncles, cousins or even passersby, there is something special about seeing a newborn baby. There is something even more holy and wonderful about the child's birth itself. When a baby is born, the family of the child is usually filled with an explosion of happiness and life. People are often brought to tears of joy and gladness, especially when the baby's birth had some challenges along the way.

Scripture shows us that there was a very special birth that took place over two thousand years ago – not just the birth of Christ, but the birth of His Church!

Luke records that on the day of Pentecost, the first 120 followers of Jesus were all together, gathered in one place. As they were worshipping, praying and reflecting on the teaching Jesus had left them, there came a sound like the rushing of a mighty wind. (Acts 2:1-4) The Holy Spirit had come with power!

Tongues of holy fire came upon them, and they began to speak in other languages as the Spirit gave them the ability! (Acts 2:4) They began to testify to the Resurrection of Jesus Christ. The same Jesus who had been betrayed, beaten, mocked and violently crucified upon a Roman cross was now alive and He had risen with great power for all to see! (Acts 2:32-33)

Since the Holy Spirit came at Pentecost, thousands of people had come for the Pentecost festival in Jerusalem. These same persons were now witnesses of the power of the Holy Spirit through these apostles. They heard the early Church crying out about how amazing God is and what God was doing! The early apostles were not speaking heavenly, unintelligible tongues at this point. These followers of Jesus, who were all from the Galilean countryside in Israel, had become speakers of international languages. These first witnesses were proclaiming the Good News of the Resurrection in tongues native to Africa, Europe, Asia, surrounding islands and the Mediterranean.

In light of the powerful coming of the Holy Spirit with signs and wonders, in light of the Spirit-filled preaching of Peter and the apostles, this multi-ethnic group of people confessed: "What should we do?" Peter and the disciples opened the doors of the Church: "Repent and be baptized all of you in the name of Jesus Christ for the forgiveness of your sins, and you will receive the gift of the Holy Spirit." (Acts 2:37-38) Luke records that on the day of the Church's birth, about 3,000 people gave their lives to Jesus for salvation.

Then, immediately after their conversion, these new, Spirit-filled believers entered the Church to be discipled: to grow in their loving relationship with Jesus. Luke records that "they devoted themselves to the apostles' teaching and the fellowship, to the breaking of bread and the prayers." The Church birthed a model of radically loving community [koinonia in Greek], awesome miracles of healing and provision, and caring for people so that none had need. Because the Church was born in the power of the Holy Spirit and love for one another, the Lord kept adding those who were joining it. (Acts 2:47)

To wrap up, the Church at Pentecost reveals the last step of preparation for our hearts to burn brightly with exciting joy, divine direction and unconditional love from Jesus: receiving the Holy Spirit with warm worship and excitement.

Take it from me: when you, your family, your church, or community does this, you will never be the same!

Heart Check Wrap-up

Key Point: Receiving the Holy Spirit with warm worship and excitement is the fourth step of preparing to live with a heart on fire.

Thoughts and Questions for Reflection:

- Have you ever experienced God's love in a way that made your heart feel warm or burst into worship? Scripture shows us that the Holy Spirit can rest on us with quiet joy like Elijah (1 Kings 19:11-13) or with loud, ecstatic praise as on the day of Pentecost. (Acts 2:1-4)

- Does your family, your community and/or your Christian community have activities that emphasize the values of the historic, apostolic church: teaching about Jesus, shared meals, prayer and fellowship?

- In what ways are you anticipating the coming of the Holy Spirit in your life?

In all these four steps, Jesus and the Early Church model for us how we need to prepare our hearts as spiritual candles. This is how we prepare for the exciting burning of the love and power of Jesus and the Holy Spirit to come afresh on our lives! Let's get our hearts ready as we close with this prayer.

Prayer: Dear Gracious and Loving God, thank you for showing me the steps I need to take to prepare my heart for your love, direction and power. Humble my heart before You and help me see Your Risen Presence. Prepare me for Your Holy Spirit, and fill me with joy when Your Spirit arrives. All these things I pray in Jesus's name.

Amen.

CHAPTER 3

Removing Fire Suppressants: Why Our Hearts Grow Cold, and What We Do About it

If you walk outside your home or go into the town or city you live in, at some point you will hear an unmistakable sound: the *whirrrrr* of a fire truck! Have you seen one before? Beyond access to water, fire trucks are equipped with different types of fire suppressants that limit the spread of fires.

In the natural realm, physical fires are destructive. But in the spiritual realm, the burning of the love, power and direction of Jesus Christ is a good thing: it's how we live with hearts on fire! But there are a few things I have found that can slow the wonderfully creative love of Jesus from burning at the center of our hearts, lives, families, institutions, Christian communities and world. What are these? Thanks for asking, Wonderful Person! They are *spiritual fire suppressants.*

Any time you have the presence of one or more spiritual fire suppressants in the heart, our hearts can grow cold, empty and numb to all that God has for us in Jesus Christ. I am a witness of this in my own life. For this reason, it's not enough just to prepare for the coming of the Holy Spirit's flame and love in Jesus in our hearts, but we have to constantly guard our hearts against the following four spiritual fire suppressants:

1. **Poisoning Our Hearts with the World's Values**
2. **Clinging To Dead Religion Instead of Christlike Love**
3. **Ignoring the Poor and Marginalized in Our World**
4. **Turning Away from the Timeless Means of Grace**

Suppressant #1: Poisoning Our Hearts with the World's Values

With both of my parents hailing from Alabama and my grandparents as well, I grew up and still am a big Alabama Football Fan. (If you are a fan of another team, I still love you with the love of Christ!) Recently, Nick Saban, the coach at Alabama responded to a journalist's question at a news conference with a bizarre but truthful quote. He said that the media's feeding his team with quotes about how good they are is as deadly and dangerous as "rat poison."[1]

His point was that the surrounding culture's attempt to make his team feel good was actually leading them down the wrong path.

Likewise, the world constantly offers each of us the spiritual rat poison of temptation. These are behaviors and attitudes which may look good on the outside but spiritually they are full of death and distraction. These temptations keep us from burning brightly with the love, direction and excitement of Jesus in our hearts and lives. If you, I and the entire human family are going to live with hearts on fire, we have to guard ourselves against this temptation. We have to resist conforming ourselves to the ways and values of a broken world. We have to stay focused on our purpose of living with the divine direction and love of Jesus that can change our lives and the world.

How do we do this? Thanks for asking, Wonderful Person! In his first major sermon, Jesus gathered with His closest friends and large crowds on a mountain in Galilee to help them understand their identity. During this "Sermon on the Mount", He calls us into an amazing new

---

[1] https://www.cbssports.com/collegefootball/news/nick-saban-believes-rat-poisonfrom-mediais-invading-alabama-players-heads/

identity, an identity that can define us and strengthen us for our purpose, throughout every generation - even today. He said first: "You are the salt of the earth" (Matthew 5:14). Did you know that salt by nature is designed to season? Jesus says you and I are designed to season this world with His love and grace. Isn't that amazing?! Here's the good news: God invites all of us to enter God's loving family through Jesus Christ, and that invitation is available to you today! Once we come into God's family, we take on this new identity. The great news is that Jesus then calls us to go and invite more people into this loving family and identity! If we lose our flavor, Jesus says we lose touch with this very purpose He gives us. So remember, you are salt. You are wonderfully distinct because God made you that way! Stand in the distinction of who God made you to be!

Jesus also says on the Mount that we are light: "You are the light of the world" (Matthew 5:14). As we follow Jesus in our own lives and with our brothers and sisters who seek to live with hearts on fire in Him, His light shines through us to illuminate the darkness in the world. God made you to shine brilliantly in this world, so let your light shine!

In other words, for us to burn with hearts on fire with the love of Jesus, we have to reject the evil influences of this world and turn away from the spiritual forces of wickedness that can poison our identity and our purpose.

Here are some of what those poisonous fire suppressants look like:

First is the poison of sexual promiscuity, immorality and exploitation. This poison is so deep in our culture that we must to stay on guard in some real ways! The world says that pleasure is found in promiscuous relationships, adulterous affairs, domestic and all kinds of sexual violence, pornographic exploitation and the heartbreaking, systemic damage of human trafficking. Like a stealthy shadow, these poisonous behaviors lurk and cling to too many places in our lives, our media, and our culture.

Thankfully, Jesus has a better way!

This is the good news, both for those who have done harm through these poisonous behaviors and those who have been harmed: healing is available for all! If you find yourself among those who have harmed or taken advantage of others because you have been seduced into this poisonous disease of sexual exploitation, here is your good news: Jesus can heal you and make you into a new person! In this newness in your heart and life, you can not only experience freedom from these damaging patterns of thinking and behavior, but you can experience power to participate in healing those who have been damaged by these behaviors. This restorative love of neighbor comes about by praying for our neighbors who have been taken advantage of, listening to their stories and modeling a protective caring love for others, just to mention a few. In his letter to the Church at Corinth Paul puts it this way: "If anyone is in Christ, there is a new creation, the old has passed away, all things are made new" (2 Corinthians 5:7). What good news! At the same time, if you have found yourself victimized by such destructive behaviors, there is good news for you as well! Jesus constantly demonstrates that He can heal what has been wounded in or among us: in body, mind, spirit and in relationship (Mark 3, John 4). Out of compassionate love, Jesus consistently defends those who have been victimized, offering them an opportunity for a fresh start and a new identity in Him. Paul says it like this in Romans 8:1, "There is now no condemnation for those who are in Christ Jesus". If you have been abused and/or taken advantage of, you are not condemned, but you are embraced wonderfully by God! (Romans 8:31-39; John 3:16-17). As you open your heart to burn brightly with God's love, you can experience divine healing in all parts of your life. You are not what was done to you; you are a beloved child of God! Again, as Paul says: "If anyone is in Christ, there is a new creation, the old has passed away, all things are made new" (2 Corinthians 5:7).

Second is the poisonous, worldly value of worshipping money. If we are honest, today's culture screams that money is the end-all-be-all of life. Whether it's on social media, the Internet or just in conversation, we can be deceived that having money, making money or simply money itself is everything in life.

Thankfully, Jesus constantly demonstrates throughout the Gospels that life is not found in an abundance of possessions or money, but in the Spirit of God (Luke 13; John 3:3). To be sure, He teaches us to be good stewards of whatever resources God has given us (Luke 16). When we do, we can use our financial and economic resources to empower our neighbors in love (see Chapter 11 for more). But He consistently warns us then and now that worshipping money is a road toward destruction. Wonderful Person, hear me: this is not because God desires us to be lacking in anything: God came that we might live life and live it abundantly! (John 10:10).

But the promises that wealth seduces us into are lies, just lies. Here's the Good News: When you put your trust in Jesus and His love, He will make sure you are never lacking in anything: you find true life, joy and provision in Him (Philippians 4:19).

Third is the poisonous, worldly value of prejudice. Sadly, no matter where we find ourselves amidst our rich ethnic, national and socioeconomic diversity in our families, personal lives, Christian communities and beyond, our culture is filled with deep prejudice even today.

All prejudice is rooted in a spiritual attitude of scarcity: that there are limits to who Jesus loves and who is a child of God. This sinful prejudice expresses itself as hatred, violence and/or discrimination against those who are different than us in gender, ethnicity, socioeconomic class, complexion, and/or education.

Thankfully, Jesus offers us a better way! He opposes this lying voice in His own ministry and instructs His disciples of every age to do the same. Jesus consistently demonstrates that the love of God both includes and transcends all flesh, as He engages women, children, and men, the poor, the wealthy and the outcast, criminals, Jews and Gentiles for the sake of God's kingdom in the earth. The apostle Peter picks up where Jesus left off and gives a wonderful model for those who would live with hearts on fire today.

In a holy dream given to Peter when he struggles with his internalized prejudice against Gentiles as a Jew, Jesus says to Peter: "What I have made clean, you must not call unclean" (Acts 10:15). The love of Christ transcends and includes children of God from all stripes, complexions, walks of life and experiences of humanity! Thanks be to God for such an amazing, life-changing love!

Finally, there is the poisonous, worldly value of the desire for fame and power. Our world says that your best life is found in the number of followers one has on Instagram, Snapchat, Twitter, Facebook or whatever the latest social trend might be. The lying voice of fame and power leads too many astray to compromise the integrity of their life.

I have seen too many people, leaders, communities, local churches and government officials fall into this trap: they compromise their integrity and the integrity of the love of Jesus in their lives to be popular, seen and recognized. But this is a seductive trap, one that the devil tried to tempt Jesus with as well. But thankfully, Jesus demonstrates that when we understand how we are intimately and lovingly seen and embraced by God, our souls are anchored in love and security (Matthew 4:1-12; Luke 1-12). The Good News is that no matter who you are, God already loves you, and there's nothing you can do about it! (Romans 5:6-9; John 3:16)

As we stay close to Jesus Christ in prayer, fasting and Christian community, we can renounce all forms of this first spiritual fire suppressant which can keep our hearts from burning with the love, joyful excitement and direction from Jesus.

Suppressant #2: Clinging to Dead Religion Instead of Christlike Love

I am not a horror show kind of guy, but I have seen TV previews for the popular show *The Walking Dead*. The show features an apocalyptic society at the end of the world where people are walking around trying to survive a plague of zombies. These zombies are people who look alive but in reality, they are dead.

In a similar way, if we cling to a religion that is rooted in empty traditions instead of clinging to the power of Jesus Christ and the Holy Spirit by faith, we can be misled to live life as spiritual zombies. That is, we can be tempted into a second spiritual fire suppressant: clinging to dead religion instead of a life-giving, Christlike love.

Jesus was constantly correcting and rebuking the Pharisees, the religious folk of his day, for this. For example, early in his ministry, several men had brought their paralyzed friend to be healed by Jesus (Mark 2:1-12). When he saw this man and his friends, Jesus spoke a word of healing into that atmosphere of faith: "Son your sins are forgiven." But the religious Pharisees were more focused on their own traditions than this man's wholeness: they questioned Jesus's authority rather than celebrating this man's healing! Pretty crazy, isn't it?

This type of Pharisaic attitude can tempt us to celebrate dead, legalistic religion instead of stewarding the precious things God has given us in our homes, our families, and our Christian communities as a channel or means of God's amazing love in our lives.

While Jesus was walking through a field of grain early in His ministry, He corrected the Pharisees with a beautiful, simple image. He said that "new wine cannot fit into old wineskins...for the new wine will burst the skins (Mark 2:21-22). The true value of a wineskin is its ability to be a vessel for precious wine. The same is true of our traditions:

they are called to be means of God's amazing love for us and for the world! If our lives, families, communities and Christian communities spend more time on rules and traditions than on seeking the Spirit of the living God, we are on the road to death: death to God and death to our purpose. If we do this, we will extinguish our availability for a fresh experience of the warm, exhilarating love and power of the Holy Spirit.

Here's how we avoid this fire suppressant: we have to evaluate every physical possession God has given us from this perspective: will this help me share the life-giving, world-changing power and love of Jesus with others? When our physical possessions and spiritual heirlooms have run through their usefulness, it is time to prayerfully move to a season of new wineskins that allows for the radically grace-filled love of Jesus to invade and saturate our lives, churches and communities afresh.

Suppressant #3: Ignoring the Poor and Marginalized In the World

When I was a little boy and a teenager, I can remember seeing my neighbors in need on the sides of roads and highways holding up signs saying: "Homeless. Please Help" or "Help Anyway You Can." Unfortunately, a variety of spiritual and economic factors keep many people in our communities, cities and world in constant impoverishment. Thanks be to God that these are the people Jesus calls precious and worthy; He commands us to care for these our neighbors. The next spiritual fire suppressant which can slow the burn of excitement, passion and love from Jesus in our hearts, families, and communities is neglecting to care for the least of these: those who are on the margins of society. Jesus faithfully demonstrated throughout the Gospels a compassionate, merciful love for the poor, the excluded, the marginalized and the sick. Moreover, He declared in Matthew 25 that "when the Son of Man comes in his glory" at his Second Coming, He will sift out the righteous and unrighteous for eternal life based on how they have treated the least of these: namely, the hungry, the naked, the sick, the incarcerated and the ethnic, social, or gendered stranger. (Matthew 25:31-46)

In my own journey, I have found we can often be tempted to share this life-changing love of Jesus with only those who look, sound, dress, vote and think like us. When we adopt such an arrogant, insular mindset, we cannot effectively share the love of Jesus with others and change the world.

But here is the Good News: when we step into the fullness of our calling to share the love of Jesus so that all types of people are set on fire with His love, we can make an amazing impact!

It makes me think of about an experience during my seminary years in Washington DC. During my third year, some of my classmates and I went on a short-term mission experience for one of our classes. We traveled to a very wooded community in the suburbs of Baltimore, Maryland. One of our seminary companions was the pastor of a mission church, a church literally planted in the middle of those woods in a trailer house. Thankfully, we had some good shoes to go see him and this Christian community!

What was so inspiring was seeing the way that this congregation was being the loving face of Christ to the unhoused and poor in the middle of the woods. This local congregation answered the call of Jesus to serve the least of these. Even as they were giving so generously, their reward was so much greater: experiencing being in joyful relationship with those who needed to know God loved them.

Likewise, if we do not answer Jesus's call to serve those on the margins of our communities and world with the love of Christ, we miss seeing the incredible life-changing love and unlimited happiness of Jesus burn in our hearts and our communities.

Suppressant #4: Turning Away from the Timeless Means of Grace

If you were camping and you needed to start a fire, what would you put on a campfire to make it grow? Logs? More fire from a lighter? If you answered yes to both, you're right! Both work wonderfully.

In a similar way, there are some spiritual lighters that bring us into an igniting experience of the powerful love of Jesus in our hearts. We call these the timeless values or timeless means of grace.[2] But turning away from these timeless means of grace has lasting consequences. Even though our hearts may initially burn with power, excitement and happiness when we first receive His love, if our hearts aren't sustained by these timeless practices, our hearts will eventually grow cold.

This is the last and most deadly spiritual fire suppressant which prevents the coming of the Holy Spirit to set our hearts, lives, families, communities and Christian communities on fire: turning away from the ancient means of grace. You can find all of these in Section II, right after this chapter!

It is my firm belief that if we return to the Lord through these means of grace, we can see the sparking of such a great, global life change! This holy, global spiritual wildfire will allow us to experience a fresh movement of people from all nations, generations, cultures and abilities burning with the love and direction of Jesus! What are

---

2   James King, Christlike Love Unit. John Wesley, Wesley's
     Sermons.

these means of grace? After the Heart Check Wrap-up below, turn to the next chapter and let's find out!

Heart Check Wrap-up

Key Points:

- Spiritual fire suppressants are attitudes and behaviors that keep us from experiencing the warm love, excitement, divine direction and joy of Jesus.

- The four key spiritual fire suppressants are poisoning our hearts with the world's values, clinging to dead religion instead of Christlike love, ignoring the poor and marginalized in the world, and turning away from the timeless means of grace.

Thoughts and Questions for Reflection:

- Which of the four fire suppressants is most distracting or tempting for you? Why do you think that is?

- Have you discovered any timeless spiritual principles that help you overcome those temptations?

Do you think any of them are the same as the means of grace in the next chapter?

Prayer: Dear God, thank you for creating me to live with a heart on fire with your love, purpose, direction and excitement. Help me not to fall into temptation, but deliver me from all things that would keep me from giving my whole heart and life to you. These things I pray in Jesus's name.

Amen.

SECTION II

Lighting the Fire: How Our Hearts Burn Bright with Excitement, Purpose and Christlike Love

Have you ever gone camping before? I can remember going camping several times as a little boy growing up in Tennessee with my church's children's ministry and later my youth group. I enjoyed being out in creation, seeing the wonder of the heavens and stars, being together with my friends and of course, making s'mores around the fire! But learning how to make a good fire came later in my life.

That lesson came when I went on a mission trip with some of my pastor friends from the Atlanta area. During our journey toward ordination we took a trip to Hinton, South Carolina to serve a family whose farm had been badly damaged by a storm. After one of our long days of work helping them rebuild, my friends and I came to hang out at the warmth of one of the fires burning at the local fire pit. The fire was warm, and the more we added logs to it, the more it burned brighter and brighter, warming us and lighting up the night sky! The more we stoked it with a fire from a lighter, the more it burned with warmth and light!

Just as those logs were lit and sustained by a fire, so Jesus Christ longs for us to burn spiritually with a living fire of the Holy Spirit: a love that is unquenchable, a direction that is eternal, and an exciting passion and purpose that is contagious. There are means of grace which like that lighter help us experience the love of Christ and usher in wonderfully new life and power into our lives, our hearts, our families, our churches and our communities so that the darkness of this world can be cast out and warmed by our hearts on fire for God, ourselves and others!

Are you ready to find out what these spiritual lighters are?

Turn the page and find out!!

CHAPTER 4

The Best Wireless Connection: Life-Giving Prayer

If there's anything that's become common to our lives today it is this: cell phones! Do you remember the first time you spoke to someone on a cell phone? Maybe it was a close friend, a family member, someone from your Christian community, or someone from a social group you are connected to. Cell phones are basically lifelines today; it is difficult to navigate a tech-centered world without them. But the quality of the conversation we have with someone is based on the strength of the signal of our phones. Even if you have a good phone, you cannot hear the person you are talking to if you have a poor connection.

Likewise, we cannot receive all of the direction, power and love that God has for us in Jesus Christ if we do not have a rich connection with God in prayer. The Good

News for us is this: prayer is the best wireless connection ever! As one of the saints who nurtured my faith would remind me: "Jesus is on the mainline, tell Him what you want!"

Prayer is simply this: our ongoing conversation with God. God longs to be in conversation with us. Best yet, we can talk with God anywhere and anytime! I can remember some of my first experiences of prayer when I was a little boy. In our home in Tennessee, I would often say my nightly prayers to God at my bedside. I can remember enjoying my conversation with God, sharing with God about my day and listening to the Holy Spirit's whispers and promptings in my soul. I can remember as well spending time in prayer with my family at home.

We had time for prayer together at the table during meals. Our prayer continued at other times as well, during joyful occasions and when there were challenges in our life and in the world. During all my formation as a follower of Jesus early in my life, God instilled in me the value of a life of prayer through the powerful influences of my family and the churches that raised me.

When we spend time with our divine Parent in prayer, God will faithfully speak to us, giving us passion, excitement and strength for our life's journey.

In the Gospels, we find that Jesus faithfully modeled the beauty and the power of a life of prayer. He was always spending time with God in prayer. Jesus would often slip away from the crowds to spend time in prayer, whether it was going to a mountainside to spend time with God or going to the Garden of Gethsemane during His most challenging moments of life. It is in prayer that Jesus experienced revelation and insight (Luke 6), the powerful anointing of the Holy Spirit to heal the sick and cast out unclean demons (Luke 4), special spiritual communion with the Father (Luke 22), as well as the joy of that closeness with God (John 14). He also in prayer found strength from God to commit the greatest sacrifice of love ever made for you and for me on the Cross! (John 3:16)

After Jesus's death and resurrection, the importance of prayer continued for those who would live with hearts on fire in His love. It was when the 120 disciples of Jesus had persevered in prayer in the Upper Room in Jerusalem that the Holy Spirit came upon them with fresh power to proclaim the Good News of the Resurrected Jesus Christ! (Acts 2:1-11) So for each of us, prayer is an essential means of grace to experience a fresh touch of God's power and love, every day and all the time.

So how is your prayer life? In ministry as a pastor, I have observed that sometimes we can overthink or overcomplicate prayer. The Good News is that prayer is simple! Again, prayer is our conversation with God: God speaks and we listen, and we speak and God listens. Jesus also reminds us of two wonderful lessons about prayer:

God already knows what we need, and God longs to talk with us. What wonderful, good news!

As shared in Chapter 2, Jesus provides us the model prayer for we who would live with hearts on fire. This is the Lord's Prayer:

> "Our Father who art in heaven, hallowed be thy name. Thy kingdom come, thy will be done on earth as it is in heaven give us this day our daily bread and forgive us our trespasses as we forgive those who trespass against us. Lead us not into temptation but deliver us from the evil one." (Matthew 6:9-13)

The Didache, a manual of Christian faith from the Early Church reminds us of the closing benediction for this prayer:

> "For thine is the kingdom, the power and the glory forever. Amen."[3]

As we seek to burn brightly with the passion, direction and love of Jesus through prayer, know that it is important to build up a daily habit of prayer in your life, in your family, and/or with those who are close to you.

---

[3]   http://www.didache.com/didache-andlordsprayer-1/

As your prayer time with God grows richer, consider gradually increasing your time of prayer with God. Take it from me: you will find yourself spending more time with the Lord in this ultimate wireless connection. You will find yourself leaving prayer renewed and strengthened with revelation, power, and excitement. Many times during my morning or evening prayer, I have risen from my knees or standing with a fresh burning of the Holy Spirit in my heart and joy for my journey.

Just like human relationships require spending time together for more intimacy, God yearns for us to spend quality time in prayer so our relationship with God can grow more intimate. This is the same whether we are new to following Jesus or if we have been following him for years. It is the same whether we are serving in a leadership role in the life of our school, friend group, home, community or Christian community or not.

When we get into the presence of God in prayer, we will hear what the Holy Spirit is saying to us, our families, our communities, our Christian community and the entire world!

Life-giving prayer is the first means of burning spiritually in our hearts with the love of God in Christ: the best wireless connection ever! Let's make time to pray and get ready for our Heart Check.

Heart Check Wrap-up:

Key Points:
- Prayer is our ongoing conversation with God.
- Jesus's prayer for the disciples is our model prayer: The Lord's Prayer.
- The more time we spend in prayer, the more we will burn with the powerful strength, love, clarity, direction and revelation of the Holy Spirit through Jesus Christ.

Thoughts and Questions for Reflection:
- How does it feel knowing that God already loves you and waits for you in prayer? Does it make you want to pray more?
- How much time do you spend in set apart prayer? If you don't have a current time frame, start with a goal of 15 minutes during the morning, midday or evening.

- Do you, your family, your Christian community, or organization have a dedicated time or ministry of prayer during the week? If not, seek to start one.

Prayer: Gracious God, thank you that you want to be in conversation with me and all your children in prayer. I'm amazed! Give me the discipline to spend time with you daily so that I can live with a heart on fire in your love. In Jesus's name I pray. Amen.

CHAPTER 5

A Soul Feast: Feeding on the Word of God

No matter who we are, do you know one thing that every single living thing needs to live? Food! Everything living in creation eats because food is essential to our lives. Food provides nourishment for our body, strengthens our health and empowers us to do what God created us to do. It also creates a space for community at the table (more on that in the next chapter). Just like food is essential for our physical health, meditating on the Holy Bible is essential for our spiritual lives. Without a doubt, I know from my own journey that the Word of God is the very bread from God that feeds our souls with true life.

So if you find yourself lost and hungry for direction, purpose and clarity, it's time to feed on the Word of God!

Jesus helps us understand this in the Gospels. Early in Matthew's Gospel, Jesus has just been baptized: He is at a mountaintop moment in His life. But immediately after that, something unusual happens: he is driven into a wilderness place, a desert place by the Holy Spirit. (Luke 4:1-13) While he is there, he denies himself of food for forty days through fasting. Afterwards, he is tempted by the devil to turn stones into bread. Jesus's response is classic. Quoting Deuteronomy, he says: "Man shall not live by bread alone but by every word that comes from the mouth of God." (Matthew 4:4)

In other words, Jesus shows us that our lives are not simply nourished by physical food alone; we need the life-giving Word of God to nourish our souls, our dreams, our relationships and guide our lives! We need living Bread, the Word of God! We receive this living bread by studying Scripture and more importantly by meditating on Scripture.

Meditating on Scripture is not the same as other ways of engaging the Word of God. Meditating on Scripture is not like preparing for a Bible study, memorizing verses for a Sunday School class, or like preparing for a lesson or a sermon.

Meditating on the Word of God is allowing the Holy Spirit to speak to us as we listen for God's voice through quiet, repeated reading and chewing on God's Word.

In my own life, a truly significant moment in my practice of feeding on Scripture came during my high school years. I attended a Youth Disciple Retreat in

Wilmore, KY with several friends from across our church's annual conference. One of the disciplines I learned during that time was meditating on the Word. During each morning of that week away at camp (I'm sure our parents were thrilled for some time by themselves!), we would go to different parts of the campus at Asbury Theological Seminary and meditate on Scripture.

After spending time cherishing God's Word in quiet or silence, we would write down any revelation and insight from God during that time. That began a life-long discipline of meditating on God's Holy Word for me. There's nothing more powerful than when we individually and collectively hear, meditate and feed on the word of the living God!

Here's why this is important: in today's culture, there is a rising fascination with meditation. Magazines and articles in stores often encourage us toward mindfulness and the like. It is good that people are seeking to be intentional about their inner lives. But there is a difference between the world's meditation and meditating on Holy Scripture. The goal of feeding on the Word of God is hearing from God in quiet and silence, not focusing on or desiring material things from the world.

Here's the Good News about this practice of meditating on the Word of God: as we meditate on the word of God that is breathed by the Spirit of God, we will be nourished and nurtured spiritually as sons and daughters of God!

It is the meditation on the eternal Word of God that will give birth to the fruit of the Spirit in our lives, the actual presence of God in our lives, our families, our institutions, our Christian communities and the world! (Galatians 5:22-23) As Jesus the Living Word Himself says: "I am the Bread of Life: whoever comes to me will never be hungry, and whoever believes in me will never be thirsty." (John 6:35) In the midst of a world where we often have constant, distracting influences pulling on us from the media, from social media, from people in our social circles, meditating on the Word of God will guide our lives into purpose, power and a clear sense of direction.

So here's how we nourish ourselves in God's Holy Word practically: Carve out intentional time in the morning, noonday or evening for quiet time with God. After asking for the Holy Spirit to speak to you in prayer, find your Scripture for your devotional time.

You can use resources below if you need help starting.[4] Read the Scripture passage slowly. Listen first for words or phrases that God brings into your spirit. Read it again. Listen then for how you hear God calling you to respond in light of this message. Consider writing it in a journal or typing it out on your favorite device. Then continue your

---

4   Upperroom.org, seedbed.com

time in prayer. The Ignatian Lectio Divina is a great model for this discipline as well.[5]

I invite you, your family, your community, your Christian community or institution to feast on the living bread of Holy Scripture in a fresh way. As you meditate on Scripture, you will find yourself nourished, refreshed and overflowing with the burning love, direction and joy from Jesus Christ. Let's get ready for the Heart Check!

---

[5] https://www.ignatianspirituality.com/ignatianprayer/the-what-how-why-ofprayer/prayingwith-scripture/

Heart Check Wrap-up

Key Points:
- The Word of God is spiritual food for our souls.
- Meditating on Scripture is listening for the voice of God through slow, prayerful and repeated reading of Scripture.

Thoughts and Questions for Reflection:
- Do you have a Bible or Bible app that you use regularly?
- Do you have set apart moments for quiet devotional time in the Word of God? If not, take time for 10-15 minutes each day in the morning, evening or night.
- Do you have a favorite Scripture in the Holy Bible? If so, why is it special to you? If not, take time to discover what Scripture speaks to you as you begin this new spiritual practice of meditating on God's Word.

- Is there a Scripture that you want to feast on more?
- How can you, your family and/or your Christian community help others grow in this way of feasting on the Word of God?

Prayer: Faithful, Holy God, thank you for the richness of Your Word. Your Word is a lamp to my feet, a light to my path, and nourishment for my soul. Give me an ear to listen for your voice by meditating on Scripture daily. Help me slow down to hear what your Spirit is saying to me and others so that we might live as your children with hearts on fire. Through Jesus Christ our Lord. Amen.

CHAPTER 6

A Happy Meal:
Celebrating Holy Communion

B e honest with me Wonderful Person: when you saw the title of this chapter, did your thoughts go to McDonald's? There's no shame if they did (smile). We likely all have had the experience of picking up a Happy Meal, either for ourselves or for the younger people in our lives. I can remember from childhood that Happy Meals always had tasty food (even if it wasn't the healthiest) along with a cool box and a toy inside. You wanted a Happy Meal because you knew that when you opened it, there would be something tasty and wonderful inside.

Whether you have experienced a Happy Meal or not, I have tasted and seen that there is a truly divine, nourishing, life giving meal that God created for all of us to share: the feast of Holy Communion.

Communion is another ancient means of grace that ignites our hearts to burn with the power, love, direction and excitement of Jesus Christ! It is the divinely happy meal because Jesus Christ is present with us at the table, offering us His Presence and His love.

I remember my first experiences of the Communion meal at my home church in Nashville, TN. Growing up, I can remember coming with fellow church members to receive the body and blood of Christ in Communion at the sanctuary's altar. We partook of the bread and the cup of Christ with great thanksgiving, great gratitude as well as seriousness. I can remember the pastor of my childhood saying after we received the meal, "Rise and go, and may the peace of Christ go with you." I can remember feeling the blessed assurance that Jesus had died for my sins and by the power of the Holy Spirit, He was living in me through the Sacrament! I was and still am blown away by the wonder of His love and the sacredness of His presence: that in this holy meal, He reminds us that He is dwelling with us and in us! Those early experiences of Holy Communion confirmed and shaped throughout my Christian journey the joy of experiencing Communion often in every season of my life. The Good News for you and me is this: Jesus is still offering Himself in this meal for all people today!

Scripture helps us understand. When Jesus gathered with His first disciples in Jerusalem at the Last Supper before His betrayal and crucifixion centuries ago, He took the bread at the table, gave thanks to God, gave it to them and said:

> "Take, eat, this is my body which is given for you. Do this in remembrance of me. And He did the same with the cup after supper, saying, This cup that is poured out for you is the new covenant in my blood." (Luke 22:14-19)

When the disciples found themselves lost, dejected and hopeless on the road to Emmaus after they felt that hope had died with Jesus's crucifixion, Jesus met them in the breaking of the bread as well. (Luke 24:13-35)

This is why Communion is a truly happy meal. It is a timeless feast where Jesus feeds us His love, grace and goodness. If you are ready for your life, your family, your community, your Christian community and beyond to be set on fire with the love of Jesus, you need to make a habit of feasting on Holy Communion often.

In Communion, we feast on the merciful grace of Christ who died for us while we were yet sinners! (Romans 5:8). While we were in our deepest, darkest moments of shame, separation, failure and disobedience, Christ died for us: what amazing grace!

In Communion, we celebrate the mighty acts of God throughout time, in the life of Israel, and in the life of Jesus Christ, giving thanks to God through Him!

In Communion, we feast on the joyful celebration of His wonderful deeds at His table! In Communion, we remember Christ's sacrifice as well as anticipating His glorious return in as we remember the words of the liturgy: "Christ has died, Christ has risen, Christ will come again."[6]

Here's one more benefit of this divinely happy meal: Communion is God's reminder that we are never too far away in failure or sin to come back home to God's love. It breaks my heart to see so many people in our world who are broken and hurting because they are lost: alienated from God, drifting in the valleys of despair, sin and hopelessness. When we receive Communion, we have the joy of experiencing ourselves and telling others that the table where Jesus Christ offers Himself is a radically grace-filled and open table. No matter who you are or what you've done, you are welcome at Jesus's table![7]

When Jesus Christ shared the first Communion (Eucharist) with his disciples, let's take a look at who was around the table. First there was Peter, the same Peter who would deny him in a few hours - yet Peter was invited

---

[6]   United Methodist Hymnal. Service of Word and Table II.
[7]   United Methodist Liturgy. Service of Word and Table II.

to Communion. Then there was Judas, who would betray him in a few moments for a few dollars and cents - yet Judas was invited to Communion by Jesus. Then there were the other disciples who would desert him at his deepest time of need (excluding John), yet - Jesus still offered them Communion.

What an eternal happiness to know that He offers us that same Communion meal freely as a gift of grace today. This is why the church's liturgy reads: "Christ invites all, all to his table, those who love him, who earnestly repent of their sin, and seek to live in peace with one another."[8]

So here is the Good News, Wonderful Person: Jesus Christ invites you, yes YOU, to His feast of Communion. No matter what you've done, who you are or are not according to what the world says, or what your past says, or what social media says, you are invited to Christ's table! No matter your experiences of rejection, failure or sin, Christ invites you to His table. Come and be healed! Come and feast on the Bread of Life! Come and enjoy Jesus, the True Bread which has come down from Heaven! (John 6:35)

At His table you can receive His greatest gift: the gift of His presence in His body and blood offered in the bread and cup. So, if you are ready to be revived with a heart

---

[8]   United Methodist Liturgy. Service of Word and Table Page 12, UMH

on fire with the love of Jesus, come to the table! Jesus is waiting. His grace is waiting. His presence is waiting. Come and Feast, and let's check our hearts while we are at it!

Heart Check Wrap-up

Key Points:
- In Communion, Jesus Christ offers us His very presence in the bread and the cup. It is a blessed, truly happy meal.
- The feast of Jesus Christ is best shared at an open table, where all are welcome.

Thoughts and Questions for Reflection:
- When you consider that Jesus shared the first Communion with people who weren't perfect and would soon deny or betray him, how does that make you see Jesus? How does it make you see the Communion meal?
- Go study each of the passages of the Lord's Supper in the Gospels (Matthew 26:24-25; Mark 14:18-21; Luke 22:21-23; John 13:21-30). How are they different? How are they the same?

- When you come to the table of Jesus in your home or in another way, meditate on Christ's forgiveness for you and invite other people, even inviting people who don't know Jesus yet, to the table.

Prayer: Gracious and Holy God, I am so thankful that you gave yourself for me in your Son Jesus Christ. Open my heart to receive your body and blood in Holy Communion so that I can experience your precious sacrifice, your wonderful love and your presence dwelling in me. As I receive Communion, make me one with Christ, one with my brothers and sisters in the body of Christ, and one in ministry to the world that all might feast at your table.[9] In Jesus Christ's name I pray. Amen.

---

[9]   Inspired by Communion Liturgy. A Service of Word and Table.

CHAPTER 7

Better Together: Being Embraced in Loving, Christian Community

No matter who we are, where we are from or what culture we call home, there is something we probably agree on: relationships are important. Very important!

Do you remember the first relationship where you felt loved? Maybe it was a parent or grandparent, maybe it was a sibling, maybe it was someone from your Christian community, maybe it was a significant other in your life. My parents, grandparents, aunts and uncles were all part of those first relationships where I felt loved. And my home church crowned those first experiences of love in my life. I felt that love anchoring me with the love of Jesus from childhood, adolescence and onward.

Regardless of where you first felt loved and embraced, loving relationships are at the heart of a wonderful, happy, joy-filled life. In each circle of relationships in our lives, among family, friends, among the community of faith and beyond, God has made us to be in loving relationship with each other. In fact, God said so at the creation of the first man and woman.

When Adam was made by God's hand and set in the Garden of Eden, God noticed that Adam wasn't fully happy; something was missing! God made Eve, the first woman, to add companionship to the life of humanity, saying, "It is not good that man should be alone." (Genesis 1:18) I'm sure Adam was a happy camper when God created Eve! I know I would be!

Solomon, the wisest person to ever live, said that "Two is better than one, because they have a good return for their labor." (Ecclesiastes 4:9-12) In a timeless way, Jesus declares to the first disciples of the early Jesus movement: "Wherever two or three are gathered in My Name, there I am in the midst of them." (Matthew 18:20) Wow, amazing!

All this brings us to the fourth timeless way that our hearts can burn with the amazing, exciting love of Jesus: being embraced in loving, Christian community.

Being together is the lifestyle for those who want to live with hearts on fire in the love of Jesus: in our own hearts, lives, families communities, institutions, Christian communities and beyond. When we come together, Jesus is present! We can experience His love, His joy, His healing,

His forgiveness, His revelation, His power and anointing.[10] But the Early Church and the early Methodist movement understood something particular about practicing Christian community. If we are going to live with hearts on fire in Jesus Christ, we have to connect intentionally and regularly with each other.

Come with me into the New Testament, where Scripture helps us understand. The Bible says that when the early Church was born on the Day of Pentecost, several things happened after the conversion of these new believers in the Jerusalem church. Luke says that "they devoted themselves to the apostles' teaching and to the fellowship." (Acts 2:42-47) Luke records that day by day these first believers spent time together breaking bread with glad and generous hearts from house to house!

In an amazing way, this was a multicultural, multilingual community, mostly of Jews with a few non-Jews included. But eventually the Church became richly multiethnic as well, seen throughout the entire New Testament. The multi-ethnic nature of the New Testament Church was seen in every single local church: at **Antioch** (Acts 11:19-20), **Corinth** (1 Corinthians 1:23-25), **Rome** (Romans 1:5, Romans 1:16), and **Ephesus** (Ephesians 3:6).

This multi-ethnic model captures the fullness of God's intention for all nations, people and generations to be set

---

10   King, Christlike Love Unit.

on fire with the love of Jesus together! (Revelation 7:9; Matthew 28:19-20)

Here's the Good News then: the love of Jesus Christ in Christian community both *includes and transcends* every human ethnic group, tribe, gender affiliation, and any other outward characteristic of humanity! What an amazing love! This love can heal the brokenness and division of our time!

In my own journey with Jesus, I have found how joyful, rich and happy I feel when in a small group of Christian community and support, no matter the group makeup or setting. My parents formed my first small group of Christian community from the time I was a little boy. While in conversation and daily encounters with them, I felt the unconditional love of Jesus Christ. Later in my journey, I found a group of fellow seminary colleagues that have become truly wonderful friends. We have formed a Christlike Love Unit together, and meet weekly via conference call for a time of love, support, and encouragement.

What makes engaging ourselves in Christian community so rich today is that technology adds so many exciting possibilities for how that connection can look. Like my friends from seminary and I discovered, we can connect with each other even though we are in different states in the US: Maryland, Texas and Georgia. Even so, though technology can supplement Christian community within our lives, families, and churches, it cannot replace real in-person Christian community as a whole. Jesus coming in the flesh is confirmation that God's will is for us to experience love through in-person experiences as well as through technology as much as possible: for "the Word became flesh and dwelt among us." (John 1:14)

If you and I are going to grow more Christlike and live with hearts on fire in the love of Jesus, we need several different layers of Christian connection in our lives. The most intimate level is reminiscent of the Wesleyan bands or the Christlike Love Units. This is a weekly small group gathering where you and 4-5 others can meet together for Christlike love, support and encouragement. You might meet in person or online for this.

We also need a Christian community that will help us grow more intentionally in the teaching and lifestyle of Jesus. These church classes or larger local fellowships within a congregation or Christian community in a home help us to grow intentionally as followers of Jesus that are empowered to change the world.

Lastly, all of us need Christian community in a local community of faith. Quite frankly, it is not possible for us to experience the beauty, joy, and excitement of life in Jesus without living together in Christian community.

So no matter what culture or generation you are from, no matter what season you find yourself in in your relationship with Jesus, you need loving Christian community around you. It's time to get connected, Wonderful Person! Because we are better together! Let's go to Heart Check so we can connect in that community!

Heart Check Wrap-up

Key Points:

- God made each of us to live in loving, Christlike community with each other.
- God's ultimate dream for any local Christian community as well as the wider church is a multi-ethnic expression of the body of Christ. (Revelation 7:9).
- In order to live with hearts on fire for Christ, each of us needs three places in Christian community:
  o The small group level: Christlike Love Unit/ band
  o The formational level: the class
  o The communal level: the local Church

Thoughts and Questions for Reflection:

- Where did you first feel the love of Christ in your life? If you have not, are you ready to get connected with a loving Christian community so you can

79

feel His love there? If so, please reach out via the resource below so we can connect you.[11]

- Are you currently engaged in a small group of Christian community? If so, what makes that Christian community special? If not, why not?

- Our Christian community should be intentionally diverse so that the Holy Spirit can sharpen us in the love of Christ with disciples of different backgrounds and life experiences. How does this leading toward a diverse, multi-ethnic community make you feel? Excited? Worried? Scared? Why?

- Is your church working toward becoming a multi-ethnic congregation? If not, why not? Here are some resources to help you when you are ready to take that journey.[12]

Prayer: Dear God, thank you for the amazing gift of your love. Thank you for how you made me to experience your love in Christian community with brothers and sisters from all walks of life, cultures and life experiences. Give me courage and commitment to stay connected with my fellow sisters and brothers so that I know that I am never alone because of Your love. In Jesus's name I pray, Amen.

---

[11] Rskheartsonfire@gmail.com
[12] Deymaz, Growing a Healthy Multi-Ethnic Church. Deymaz and Okuwobi, Multi-Ethnic Conversations.

CHAPTER 8

A Joyful Noise: A Life of Worship

Wonderful Person, no matter who we are, when people see us, they see a reflection of the communities and life experiences that have shaped us.

One thing that most people eventually find out upon meeting me is that I am a son of a pastor and a Christian bishop. Growing up with this heritage of faith, and now as a man who is a pastor myself, I am often asked the same question by many people: what was it like growing up in a pastoral and episcopal family? I often have the same response for those who ask: I went to church a lot!

But beyond Sunday worship, my rearing as a follower of Jesus whose heart has been set on fire in Christ's love has included worship beyond Sundays. Since my Dad would often be away some weekends for preaching engagements and ministry work during my teenage years, we would often set aside time as a family to worship the Lord our God at home.

Each time we gathered, we would come into the living room and begin with prayer. Someone would read a Scripture from the Bible, and then we would sing a Christian song: a hymn, spiritual or some current song. After reading the Scriptures, one of us would share from Scripture what we heard as the Holy Spirit led us to give insight on the Word of God. We would sing another song, share our hearts and finish our time. This was often how we entered into the presence of God as a family, and that legacy has had such an amazing impact on me. It has blessed my soul!

Even more, I can remember during the week together, we would sing Christian songs, hymns and spiritual hymns to God throughout the day. (Ephesians 5:19) To be sure, we listened to other music as well (jazz, R&B, hip hop, pop music and Michael Jackson, which is its own category). But we would always come back to Christian music, whether it was Pentecostal-like praise, gospel, holy hip hop, Christian contemporary music, Southern hymns, or for me, international praise in Spanish or other languages.

Beyond worship as a family, I also experienced worship during the week in powerful ways at Christian music festivals. *Ichthus* was one such festival that took place just outside Wilmore, KY. For several days during the springs of my teenage years, my church's youth group and I would travel for a fun time of worshipping God, coming closer to Jesus, and enjoying the adventure of camping outside in the green fields of God's creation.

All these special moments with family and with Christian friends rooted me in the fifth timeless means of God's grace. This channel of the life-changing love of Jesus is often neglected by many individuals, families, Christian communities, and entire generations: it is worship beyond Sunday mornings. It is living a life of worship.

When talking about worshipping God, I have found worship is often only talked about in the context of the collective Christian worship experience on Sunday mornings. But from my life and the life of the New Testament Church, I have found that living with hearts on fire with Jesus's love means experiencing that love beyond the Lord's day in worship.

Worship is not something we do only on one day a week! Worship is something God desires to become a regular part of our lives, the life of our families and in the world! When we get into the presence of God regularly during worship, something amazing can happen!

When we worship the Lord with our friends, families, in our homes, in our schools, and on our jobs outside of Sunday mornings, the Holy Spirit begins to shift the atmosphere of our lives from emptiness to fullness, love, joy, peace and fulfillment. (John 12:1-8) As the Apostle

Paul says: worship helps experience the fullness of the love of Christ so that we might be "filled with all the fullness of God." (Ephesians 3:16-19)

The Early Church helps us to understand in the book of Acts. When the Holy Spirit fell upon the apostles on the day of Pentecost, the Bible records that the crowds gathered in Jerusalem that day heard a happy, joyful noise. The Holy Spirit fell in ways that caused the apostles to joyfully proclaim the Resurrection of Jesus Christ! (Acts 2:1-12)

Later in Acts, when Paul and Silas had entered one of their missionary adventures for the Gospel in Philippi of Asia Minor, their ministry included healing a young woman who was possessed by a spirit of divination and held under captivity by slave owners. When they set her free in the name of Jesus, the people of that town hated them because those citizens were more concerned about money than her healing. But when Paul and Silas were thrown in prison, thankfully that wasn't the end of the story. They started to sing and worship God in the jail cell: wow!

When they began to worship God outside of the time of regular "church" service, God sent an earthquake that shook the foundation of the prison and released them all! (Acts 16) Moreover, that supernatural worship experience opened the door for new people to receive the gift of salvation and the love of Jesus Christ! So, since worship is powerful, let's not reserve it only for Sunday mornings!

The early Methodist movement understood this as well, because it was known as a singing community. Charles Wesley often wrote many songs on horseback, not in the church proper, but in the sanctuary of God's creation. The songs of Zion[13], the anthems of the historically African American church, Christian Contemporary music, international praise and modern hymns reflect music that brings us into the presence of God beyond our worship on Sundays. Today, the rich variety of Christian music spans multiple genres: from modern worship, urban praise, classic anthems, holy hip hop and many different linguistic tongues even in the American church.

So how is your worship life? Have you sung to God recently? No matter where you are in your relationship with Jesus, I invite you to draw closer to Him through singing more, whether you are at school or home, on your job, at the gas station, or out and about in your community or city. It is our worship that brings us more regularly into the presence of God. It is worship that brings our hearts into the burning love, joy, passion and excitement of the Holy Spirit in Jesus's name. It is worship that helps us share this overflowing love with others.

---

[13]   Songs of Zion, Abingdon Press.

In the coming days, I encourage you to sing or write a new song to God in worship as you reflect on God's goodness in your life. Then watch how you, your family, your community, Christian community and others around you will be filled with hearts on fire with God's love! Let's sing and then go to heart check!

Heart Check Wrap-up

Key Points:

- Living a life of worship is the fifth timeless means of grace.
- Worship is not something that is limited to being in a building on Sundays: worshipping God is something we are called to do every day!
- No matter what genre or language of music appeals to you, you can worship God through that style, genre and tongue! (Acts 2:11)

Thoughts and Questions for Reflection:

- How might you make time each day for worship that brings you into the presence of God?
- Have you ever had "home-church" with your family or friends in person or on a technology call? If not, imagine how that might look to have a time of prayer, Scripture reading and singing together.

- Read and/or sing the Psalms as a part of your devotional time. Then write your own psalm of praise and worship to God.

Prayer: O Holy and Good God, thank you for Your wonderful Presence. Thank you for reminding us that In Your Presence is fullness of joy. (Psalm 16) Help me take time to praise you and worship you beyond Sunday morning worship. Empower me with all your children to praise You when I am feeling low and am feeling high. All glory and honor belong to You. In Jesus's name. Amen.

SECTION III

Spreading the Fire: Changing the World by Loving Our Neighbors

I magine this with me: while outside camping on a cold night, you discover a burning fire. After coming around this fire, your body and your entire life are brought to life with its light and wonderful warmth. But after leaving the fire to return to your tent, you discover that someone else outside doesn't know about this fire. In fact, there is a whole community of people living outside who have not been exposed to this life-warming fire. Wouldn't you want them to experience the same warmth, life and excitement you just experienced? I know I would!

In a similar way, when our hearts begin to burn with the excitement, divine direction, and amazing love of Jesus, His powerful love and joy is so great that we can't keep it to ourselves. Living with hearts on fire in the love of Christ means being compelled to share this love and excitement like a fire that bubbles over and catches on: a holy wildfire that has the power to change the world!

In other words, the more we experience the life-giving, exciting love of Jesus in our own hearts and lives, God will send us to share this love with our neighbors all around us: in our schools, our communities, our families, our workplaces and businesses, our Christian communities, and our institutions to the ends of the earth. This is spreading the fire: changing the world by loving our neighbors so that all people on earth can live with hearts on fire for God, self and others.

Jesus says it simply and beautifully in the Gospel of Matthew this way: "the greatest Commandment is to love the Lord your God with all your heart, soul, mind and strength, and a second is like it: to love your neighbor as yourself." (Matthew 22:38-40) Likewise, the apostle John says this: "You cannot say you love God whom you do not see and not love your brother or sister whom you see every day." (1 John 4:20)

There are four timeless practices of mercy and justice that launch us to spread the love of Christ we have received into our world. So if you are ready to change the world, keep reading so we can spread this holy wildfire!

CHAPTER 9

Stand Up And Walk!
Healing Our Neighbors

Getting electrocuted is never the way you plan to start a Saturday morning. But that's the way one Saturday started for me in my mother's beauty salon when I was a little boy. My mother and my grandparents ran a beauty salon in Nashville, Tennessee for many years. This particular morning, my boyish adventures in the salon went to a new level: placing a hair pin in a live electrical outlet. Needless to say, I was shocked by the pain of that lesson! But thankfully I was soothed by the healing comfort of my mother's tender love!

Do you remember the first time someone helped you heal after you were wounded or sick?

Maybe it was a parent, sibling or grandparent who picked you up after you skinned yourself on the playground. Maybe it was someone who held you to soothe a broken heart when you had to move to a new city, a new home or a new relationship. Maybe it was a friend who prayed for you when it felt like your mind was broken with anxiety and stress. I can remember many of those moments throughout my life.

Regardless of your first time experiencing pain and soothing, the reality is this: all of us break. Our bodies, minds, and souls are fragile and must be handled with care. But here is the Good News: in the midst of the brokenness we experience spiritually, mentally, relationally, and physically in our lives, Jesus is the Master Healer! As we follow Christ each day, He knows how to heal our lives.

But do you know the best part? As you and I follow Jesus in our daily decisions and behaviors, He sends the Holy Spirit that empowers us to bring healing to others in His name as well. Jesus Himself says to the apostles in the Upper Room, "Greater works shall you do." (John 14:14) This is Good News, because our world is in need of this.

When we look at the world today, the great cry for healing and wholeness is undeniable. The COVID 19 virus of 2020 caused a devastating chaos that shook the foundations of the world for years to come. The rise in disease, both mental and emotional dis-ease, throughout our homes and communities is alarming. The trends of how chronically debilitating sicknesses like obesity, diabetes, cancer, and other diseases are becoming more common should wake us up! This is the time — this is the season for us to stand up and walk into wholeness! This is the time to invite ourselves and those are around us into the miraculous healing power of Jesus Christ.

Come with me into the Gospel, where Scripture helps us understand. In one of my favorite passages in Mark's Gospel, Jesus has begun His ministry in Galilee. (Mark 2:1-12) The crowds begin to gather around Him from all over the region; people are so desperate for healing that they bring to the disciples many people to be healed by Jesus from sunup to sundown.

When Jesus returns home to Capernaum after His first preaching and healing tour throughout the Galilean area, He comes to his home base of operations: Peter's house. When He returns, He is crushed on all sides in the house by people seeking to hear the Word. Suddenly, some men who have a paralyzed friend take the roof off of Peter's house and lay down their friend on a mat in front of Jesus. (I wonder if Peter sent them a bill to replace his roof?!)

When Jesus sees this man paralyzed in his body, He goes to work. He says: "Son, your sins are forgiven." Stop right there! If we are going to experience the wholeness that God offers us in Jesus Christ and longs to release through our lives so we can heal our neighbors, we have to understand this first principle of healing: Healing flows from the inside out.

One of the lessons the Lord has shown me over time is that God has designed human beings as holistic beings.

We are integrated in spirit, flesh (body) and mind. Because of this, what affects one part of us will affect the rest of us. When something is not right in your body, it will cause dis-*ease* in your mind. When something is not right in your spirit, it will cause dis-ease in your body. This is why Jesus often prescribes a spiritual cure for a physical sickness. This understanding is crucial if we are going to be strong vehicles for the power of Christ to flow in us and through us to bring healing into the lives of those around us.

Healing begins in the spiritual realm! Healing begins with God because God is the author of life and wholeness: God made us (Genesis 1:27-31). When anyone has not come into a right relationship with God in Jesus Christ, they are dwelling in sin. This spiritual state of separation keeps them from wholeness and brings them into brokenness. This collective brokenness manifests in our relationships, our identities, our bodies, our hearts and our institutions in society. In this situation of brokenness in Mark 2, Jesus prescribes forgiveness for the healing of a physical condition, including the healing of this man's faith. After he was healed in his relationship with God, this man was able to "stand up, take his mat and go home" (Mark 2: 1-12).

We must all be mindful that everyone needs to first receive the forgiveness of Jesus to become a healing agent of Christ in the world. We cannot offer someone else what we have not first received. As Jesus says, "Freely you have received; freely give. (Matthew 10:8) Forgiveness is healing and liberating!

Medical research, including studies conducted by John Hopkins University, has named that forgiveness helps people by lowering their blood pressure, reducing anxiety, strengthening their immune system and helping them get good rest.[14] John Wesley, the founder of the Methodist movement, long understood and appreciated this vital link between spiritual and physical healing. He wrote a book, Primitive Physick, as a practical guide for healing physical ailments in his time.

So again, if we are going to live into healing practices that bring us and others into the wholeness of God, we have to understand the integrative nature of how God has created human life.

But there's more! The ministry of healing which Jesus invites us into as we live with hearts on fire with His power and love does not extend only to physical healing and emotional healing but also to supernatural healing as well.

Thankfully, Jesus lived this ministry of supernatural healing and gave it to the Church as well. Early to midway through His ministry, Jesus sends the twelve apostles on their first mission trip in Mark 6. (I wonder if they

---

14   https://www.hopkinsmedicine.org/news/public ations/johns_
      hopkins_health/summer_2014/the_healing_power_of_forgive-
      ness

packed flashlights!) After Jesus gives them instructions, He gives them "authority over the unclean spirits." The Bible says that their mission trip was successful, because they powerfully cast out many demons and healed many people. It makes me think of a powerful experience that happened during worship one Sunday in my ministry.

During my first season at a church I previously served, the Holy Spirit prompted me to conduct a healing service at the end of worship one Sunday. I had participated in healing services at our church's annual conference, but I had never led one myself. I could have never imagined the power of God that was about release into individuals, our congregation and community that day! Let me tell you the story.

After finishing my sermon and inviting people to the altar to receive Christ or join our church, I added a third invitation. I pleaded that those who needed healing should come down to the altar in the church's sanctuary as well. I thought there might be 2-4 people who would come down. When people started coming down en masse I was shocked! My church's leaders and ministers came down to hold me up because our healing service lasted for an hour!

I anointed people with oil and prayed over them in the name of Jesus. I saw people fall to the floor under the leadership of the Holy Spirit as they were being delivered of unclean spiritual and emotional problems. I saw people who had walked into the sanctuary with canes, feeble and slowly, be healed and set free from their ailments so they walked away without canes! I felt the Holy Spirit flow through me into those who received prayer like a high voltage electric wire!

As amazing, holy and/or unbelievable as this may sound to you, this healing power of the Holy Spirit is available to all of us today. The same power that allows us to enter into wholeness and invite others into the wholeness of God is available in the name of Jesus Christ!

Wonderful Person, I believe with all my heart and soul that Jesus Christ desires for all people to live in wholeness. Likewise, He desires that we whose hearts are set on fire in His love become His instruments of healing today around the world so that all would live in emotional, physical, spiritual and relational wholeness.

In the midst of communities that are ravaged by disease, mental health challenges, and emotional brokenness, I believe that Jesus is sending you and I to heal our neighbors by listening to our neighbors patiently, anointing our neighbors with oil and laying holy hands upon them for the power of God to enter their hearts and lives.

In the aftermath of COVID-19 that has the world living on edge, I believe Jesus is sending you and me to heal our neighbors by caring for them and offering them space to grieve and receive the comforting grace of Jesus Christ.

In the midst of broken wellness systems in society that prioritize making money rather than promoting wellness in the bodies, minds and souls of precious children of God, I believe Jesus is sending you and me to heal our neighbors. In this way, we can demonstrate a healing compassion and lifestyle in the world that values human wholeness.

So, are you ready to experience the healing power of Jesus? Are you ready to allow His healing power to flow through you? If so, let's go into Heart Check to find out more.

Heart Check Wrap-up

Key Points:

- God's desire for every human being is wellness and wholeness: physically, spiritually, relationally and supernaturally.
- One of Jesus's key ministries on earth was a ministry of healing. The Bible says Jesus healed people of *all* **diseases.** He gives this same power of healing to those who believe in Him.
- When we burn with hearts on fire with His love and excitement, Jesus sends us to be healers in our communities and our world.

Thoughts and Questions For Reflection:

- Why do you believe that Jesus had to give "authority" to the disciples to cast out unclean spirits? (Mark 6)
- What are some ways that your physical lifestyle can help nourish your overall wholeness? Could it involve your diet, exercise, and/or nutrition?

- When you think about sin as a woundedness that separates you from God, do you see the connections between spiritual and physical sickness? Do you see how the experience of salvation ushers in healing for all human life?
- Has God ever used you to heal someone in Jesus's name? Name that experience. If not, how does the possibility of being an instrument of that healing power make you feel?
- Do you have questions or anxieties about being an agent of healing for your neighbors? What are they? Get in touch with us at rskheartsonfire@gmail.com for more.

Prayer: Heavenly Father, I thank you that your desire is for me to be whole and for all of your children to be whole. Thank you for sending Jesus to heal us and make us healers. Make me an instrument of your healing so others around me may be whole, so that your entire world may be whole. In Jesus's name I pray. Amen.

CHAPTER 10

Loaves and Fishes:
Feeding Our Neighbors

Wonderful Person, I believe that there is one thing we both have in common. Can you guess what it is? We have a favorite food! My favorite food is salmon, how about yours? No matter who you are, where you are from or what your life's journey has been, there is one thing we all enjoy doing at some level: eating! God made us to eat and enjoy breaking bread together, with our loved ones, our family, and with our neighbors.

Unfortunately, although God has created a world in which there is enough food to eat from God's abundant creation, too many people go without nutritious life-giving meals each day, sometimes for many weeks or months. Greedy persons, businesses and values of greed in our culture often create situations where too many families face food insecurity on a regular basis. Entire communities, often the poor and/or ethnically minority communities, sadly experience the deprivation of quality, life-giving foods in what are called food deserts.

Thankfully, there are many whose hearts burn bright with the compassionate love of Jesus who step in to fill this hunger gap in communities and cities around our nation and world. I can remember serving in such an effort in my hometown growing up. My home church, Clark Memorial United Methodist Church, had and still has a powerful feeding ministry: Meals on Wheels. I can remember as a little boy participating in this ministry. During the week, members from our church would come and prepare meals. We would then go out in teams to feed our neighbors in the community surrounding our church. Even as we fed them, we were feeding them more than physical food; we were feeding them the love of Christ and building relationships in which the presence of God could flourish! It richly inspired and shaped me as a man, a Christian and as a pastor to this day. Our ministry was based on the life and example of Jesus Christ. Jesus, the very Bread of Life (John 6:35), constantly modeled concern for the physical hungers of people and meeting those needs throughout His ministry.

Come with me into the Gospel, and let's see what Jesus has to say about feeding the hungry in our time. On a hillside in Galilee many years ago, Jesus had just finished getting a breather from work. You see, Jesus had sent the disciples off on their first mission trip throughout the Galilean area. Now they had come back with great testimonies and celebration!

But Jesus was ready for a break - true Sabbath rest. Yet before he can get away, here come the crowds! Mark records in his Gospel, that when the people saw the disciples, they followed them *on foot* to get to Jesus and the twelve. The sun was setting and the disciples wanted to send the crowds away so they could get something to eat. But there was a problem: they were in a deserted place. There was no Whole Foods in the desert. There was no Uber Eats, Door Dash, McDonald's, Chick-Fil-A or (fill in your favorite restaurant) in the desert.

Seeing this, Jesus asks the disciples what they have. Andrew goes and finds a little boy who has a few loaves of bread and a few fish. When the disciples bring these Mediterranean Lunchables items to Jesus, they respond "What are they among so many?" (John 6:9) Jesus then took the loaves and the bread in his hands: something was about to happen!

Stop right there: this is good news here! When we think about the great needs of hunger in our communities and nation, sometimes we can get discouraged like the disciples, wondering aloud: Lord, are my gifts enough? Can my life make a difference to feeding hungry people? The Good News is Jesus says yes! When the disciples gave their gifts of food to Jesus, He took the loaves, lifted them to God, broke them and gave them to the disciples to give to all the people. To sum up, Jesus can take our gifts and resources to feed those who hunger around us.

We can share the same hope for feeding those around us today. Personally, I have observed that food insecurity is not a matter of an overall shortage of food in the world. God has made enough food for everyone in creation! So what gives with food insecurity? First, many times, you and I can overindulge in food and become wasteful in the food we buy. According to a food consumption watchdog group in America, over 40% of prepared food is wasted throughout the country.[15] How alarming! Personally, I have seen this in grocery stores and restaurants: large amounts of food being thrown away daily. That food could be used to feed the most vulnerable among us!

So Wonderful Person, practicing a ministry of feeding can begin with disciplining how much we eat ourselves. The Lord has worked on me in my own life in this area. I encourage you to watch how much food you and your family eat and buy no more. This also echoes of the lesson of the manna in the wilderness during Israel's journey in Exodus 18: When God rains bread from heaven, God is not wasteful. We see that in this feeding of the 5,000 as well.

---

[15] https://foodprint.org/issues/the-problemoffood-waste /#easy-footnote-bottom-1-1309

At another level, you might consider how you, your family, your Christian community or others could start or participate in a practice of food gleaning in your community. In the times of ancient Israel, God instructed Israel to leave the outer bands of grain and crop fields bare. In other words, God told Israel to leave them bare so that the poor in the community could have something to eat:

> "When you reap the harvest of your land, you
> shall not reap to the very edges of your field, or
> gather the gleanings of your harvest. You shall
> not strip your vineyard bare, or gather the fallen
> grapes of your vineyard; you shall leave them
> for the poor and the alien: I am the Lord your
> God." (Leviticus 19:9-10).

This is called "gleaning". Many ministries today, like St. Andrews, have great resources for such a gleaning type of food ministry.[16]

Let's get back to the miracle of feeding the multitudes. Andrew receives from the little boy what seems to be an unbelievably small offering to help feed this great crowd. Although this miracle is traditionally called the feeding of the 5,000, that 5,000 only includes men. With the women

---

[16]   https://endhunger.org/gleaning-network/

and children, it was more likely between 10,000-15,000 people to feed! That's a lot of catfish, grouper and salmon!

Jesus then takes what seems to be an unbelievably small amount of food, lifts it to God, blesses the loaves and fish and gave it to the disciples to set before the people (Mark 6:42).

The Bible says that not only did all eat and become satisfied, but also that there were 12 baskets full of broken pieces and fish! Jesus gave them leftovers for Sunday dinner!

So be comforted in this Good News, Wonderful Person: God has placed enough food in creation for us to feed everyone in our communities, including the poor. We just need to take the resources we have and place them in Jesus's hands. Then we can truly feed the world! Are you ready to find out how? Then let's move to our Heart Check time!

Heart Check Wrap-up

Key Points:

- Feeding is a ministry Jesus embraced and commands those who follow Him to continue. (Mark 6:30-44; Matthew 25:31-46)
- God has enough food in creation if we practice self-control and share with the needy, in our own lives, our families, our businesses, our Christian communities and beyond.

Thoughts and Questions for Reflection:

- How can you practice more self-discipline personally or in your family with how much food you buy? Is that easy to do or does it require more intentionality? Why?
- What are some local resources available for feeding those who hunger in your community?
- After assessing food sharing resources in your community, how can you partner with an existing

ministry, agency or food bank to create sustainable options for healthy food in your community and beyond? How might you dream of creating a new avenue of empowering, healthy food options in your community if one does not exist?

Prayer: Gracious, Creator God, thank you for creating a world where there is enough food and sustenance for everyone. Forgive me, forgive us, when we take more than we need. Give me the faith to share my food with the poor and the hungry around me. Help those who burn with hearts on fire with Jesus's love to share what we have so that all may feast. All these things we ask in the mighty name of Jesus Christ, the Bread of Heaven. Amen.

CHAPTER 11

Let My People Go:
Empowering our Neighbors
through Jubilee Economics

Have you ever made plans for summer vacation before? For many of us, vacation plans might include going to the beach, spending time with family and friends you haven't seen in a while, or just relaxing and enjoying the crisp night air and long summer nights. Going to jail usually isn't high on our summer to-do list, but several years ago, that's exactly where I went one summer.

On the outskirts of Nashville, TN, there is a maximum-security prison called Riverside. I went inside this prison, not because I had committed a crime, but to be in conversation and community with those who had. I went inside with companions from a ministry cohort I was a part of. As the bars clanged open and shut behind us, I didn't know what was in store. But it was a powerful, life-changing experience I had that day. I was blessed to meet and talk with persons who had committed some serious crimes. Thankfully, many of them had begun to experience real change in their behaviors and attitudes. I witnessed how the Lord was reforming and making new creatures out of these men.

Even so, beyond the shining hope of their own transformation, there was a larger shadow looming throughout the prison complex. That summer, I began to learn about a larger trend which undergirds the criminal justice and prison systems. Like weeds that creep up and choke life from plants, the greed-filled motives of many wealthy persons and companies in society had perverted the original vision of the corrections system. The institution of prisons, which were originally intended to reform and correct offenders, had become perverted into a profit-making business. I learned that the greed which is worshipped in our culture often entraps innocent people and overwhelmingly innocent and minority communities into pipelines that take advantage of their labor for selfish gain.

As shared in Chapter 2, Jesus Christ long recognized the dangers of greed. He recognized the way in which greed can become a spiritual fire suppressant that keeps us from living with hearts on fire in love for God and for our neighbors. He says very explicitly to the disciples in the Gospels: "No one can serve two masters…for they will either love one and hate the other, or despise one and love the other. You cannot serve both God and mammon [greed]." With even more emphasis, Paul writes to his mentee Timothy in the New Testament:

> "The love of money is the root of all evil."
> (1 Timothy 6:11)

The worship of money not only keeps us from giving our best love and commitment to God, but greed also tempts us to sin against our neighbor. It lies to us by deceiving us that harming and taking financial advantage of our neighbor is right as long as we get paid.

We commit this sin when we take advantage of vulnerable persons by lying and cheating. Our nation commits this sin when it turns the other way as the prison industrial complex plagues the criminal justice system and many minority and other vulnerable communities for the sake of profit. Companies and businesses commit this sin when they take advantage of children for the sake of profit through child labor. We commit this sin in our culture when our greed and consumptive habits have no self-control: when our desire for material things robs people of their holidays and family time because they have to work multiple jobs just to put food on their table. We commit this sin when we allow lust to pervert our vision of human beings so that we see them as as objects of our own desire instead of those made fearfully and wonderfully as children of God. We commit this sin when we allow our lust to give birth to sexual exploitation through human trafficking and rampant violence. *No matter which social ill we face in today's culture, whether civil engagement and voting, criminal justice, modern day slavery, educational disparities, access to affordable housing without predatory lending, food insecurity, student loan debt, quality health care, etc., every single institution and person in society suffers when greed is our ultimate goal.*

In light of this, you may be asking: is there hope? Is there a roadmap toward restoration and freedom? Yes! Thanks be to God that Jesus shows us a way forward. Jesus shows us how we can break free from this persistent stronghold of greed. Jesus shows us a way that we can manage the financial and economic resources God has given us to empower our neighbors and bring healing to the world. Jesus shows us how to set the oppressed free, liberating those who have been trapped by cycles and generations of unpaid labor. This practice of loving our neighbors by empowering them economically is the practice of Jubilee.

Come with me into the Gospel of Luke, where Scripture helps us understand. When Jesus begins His ministry with His first sermon in Luke 4, He invokes the prophet Isaiah. Jesus declares in this small-town synagogue of Nazareth: "The Spirit of the Lord is upon me, because

He has anointed me to preach good news to the poor, to proclaim liberty to the captives, and….to proclaim the year of the Lord's favor" (Luke 4:16-18). This year of the Lord's favor is the year of Jubilee.

The Old Testament reveals this amazing, healing economic practice. During the time of ancient Israel, God prescribed Jubilee as a wonderful way of honoring the Sabbath. Sabbath at its heart was the instruction God gave through Moses that Israel was to spend one day a week in worship and rest. But Sabbath also gave Israel an opportunity to give rest to those who labored on their behalf. (Exodus 20:8-11) This same principle was extended to Jubilee.

Every seven years, Israel was to let the land rest so that the earth could be set free from an unending cycle of planting and harvesting. This is called the Sabbath year. Jubilee is the culmination of seven Sabbath years. God says that after the seventh seven-year time period has passed, the 50th year shall be a year of Jubilee.

Listen to this amazing instruction that God gives:

> "If any who are dependent on you become
> so impoverished that they sell themselves to
> you, you shall not make them serve as slaves.
> They shall remain with you as hired or bound
> laborers. They shall serve with you until the year
> of Jubilee. Then they and their children with

> them shall be free from your authority; they
> shall go back to their own family and return
> to their ancestral property" (Leviticus 25:39-41).

Wow! Jubilee was and is a dimension of time when debts are cancelled and the enslaved go free.

Jesus lived this principle of economic empowerment and healing throughout His ministry as well. His healing set many people free not just from physical sickness, but empowered them for economic wholeness as well. (Mark 1, Mark 2) Jesus models for us God's desire in Jubilee: God desires for everyone in our families, communities, businesses, nation and world to experience *rest*. This rest is not just a physical rest, but a rest from values of greed so that we can move into the healing rest of God's generosity and love. (Galatians 5:22-23)

Now, if we are honest, when we look around and see how widespread greed is in our time, we might get a bit overwhelmed. How might you, your family, employer, business, Christian community, or institution start living into this practice of economic empowerment and rest so we can set our neighbors free? Thank you for asking, Wonderful Person!

No matter whether you are a student, employee, employer, church leader or consumer, no matter whether you steward a business, organization, your family budget or simply your grade school allowance, there a few

life-changing ways we can live out Jubilee principles in
our lives.

1. Embracing Kingdom Abundance and Generosity

The first step in living into the practice of Jubilee
individually and collectively with our communities and
beyond is understanding the importance of Kingdom
abundance and generosity. This is the foundation of any
good practice of financial and economic stewardship.

Scripture helps us understand in the book of Genesis.
When God first created the heavens and the earth, God
made a world with abundance in it and God called this
world good. (Genesis 1) Moreover, when God created
humanity, God gave us a command of stewardship and
generosity. God said: "Be fruitful and multiply, fill the
earth and subdue it." (Genesis 1:27-31) The second account
of creation in Genesis 2:15 reveals what this dominion
actually looks like: it looks like caring responsibility.
Scripture says: "the Lord God took the man and put him
in the garden of Eden to till it and keep it."

In other words, God has entrusted the natural realm
to us to steward and take care of it. Everything that we
have in life is ultimately a gift from God. Out of that
understanding of God's great abundance and how
generous God has been to us, we are to steward our personal
finances, economic resources, businesses and institutions

in a way that glorifies God by honoring and empowering our neighbor generously. This understanding is radically different from the popular, selfish understanding from our culture. When we operate in our own lives, school lives, work lives, churches and businesses with Kingdom generosity, *the goal of our personal, financial, business and collective economic life is no longer focused on who can make the most money.* Instead our goal becomes: who can steward what God has given them in ways that best empower those around them? This is the case whether our neighbors are our classmates, co-workers, our employees, our business associates, or simply our fellow citizens in community and country.

Embracing Kingdom abundance and generosity means we value giving more than taking, blessing others more than blessing ourselves. In a wonderful way not only is this more pleasing to God, but this also makes those around us more successful: whether they be our co-workers, classmates, employees, businesses and institutions. Although there are many examples, including some from my family's own experience, a current example of Chick-Fil-A is a great model. Chick-Fil-A is generous in making sure its employees have Sundays off, work in a good environment and have fair wages. This model of generosity and care ensures that people want to work there.[17] When we value giving to others because we recognize God has given to us, we can make a huge financial and collective economic impact in the lives of those around us.

2. Fasting from Unjust Practices and Businesses

In recent years, I have seen an inspiring trend in our economy. Many people have been intentional in becoming more thoughtful consumers. To be specific, many customers have become more conscious about the businesses they patronize to promote healthy, life-giving practices of labor and business.

Herein is a second step of empowering our neighbors through Jubilee economics: becoming more intentional about the companies you shop from or your church, organization or business does business with. If you come into awareness that vendors that you patronize are engaged in harmful labor practices, intermittently or totally deny doing business with them.

You can do so until they acknowledge their wrong and elevate their concern for their workers. You can alternatively find an entirely new organization or business to work with. Or, you can work to create your own business based on Jubilee principles! I recently had to do this on a

---

17   https://www.chick-fil-a.com/careers/culture

personal level. This "corporate fasting" was inconvenient for my shopping, but I wholeheartedly believe it helped myself and others grow in loving our neighbors.

A few years ago, I discovered that one of the companies that packages strawberries I love makes its workers work for extremely low wages. After learning this, I was hurt and decided to make a small but important change. I would no longer buy from this company. After sharing this need to practice a more just economic love of neighbor at a grocer where I shopped recently, a staff person at that grocer actually provided alternative options for produce outside this company at that grocer! This way more people could shop in ways that edify their neighbors, not take advantage of them. Praise God!

On an individual, church-wide, business or community scale, this signals to companies that those who are burning brightly with the love of Jesus love God and our neighbors more than we love money. It sends a refreshing, spiritually revolutionary message to the world: we can care for others instead of taking advantage of them. This is why history demonstrates the power of mass economic fasting, also called boycotts, are extremely effective in producing change.

Lastly, if God has put you in a position of leadership, whether in a business, an organization, or a Christian community, do your part in making sure that people who are employed for your organization are paid fairly.

As Jesus says in Luke's Gospel: "The worker is due their hire." (Luke 10) This is how we love our neighbors for their economic benefit and empowerment.

3. Modeling Sabbath: Refraining from Economic Activity One Day A Week

Growing up with parents from Alabama, my father would tell me of a world that seemed like a galaxy far, far away. In my father's hometown of Ashland, AL, the entire town shut down on Sundays when he was growing up. Not only did the community worship God at church but the businesses shut down as well. As a child and even now as an adult, this wholesome practice of Sabbath has inspired me and encouraged me to find out the beginnings of this practice. Ready to find out?

Several centuries ago throughout the North and the South in the US, there was a particular set of laws passed in many states. These laws, established for many years, were called **Blue Laws.** They mandated that in accordance with Holy Scripture, on Sundays, businesses, shops and stores were to be closed. This biblical trend of economic Sabbath one day a week on Sundays lasted for about two hundred years. But in the second half of the 20th century, those laws began to be erased. As they were erased, so were the benefits of economic Sabbath: rest for families, rest in the presence of God in worship, and rest for our businesses and collective means of production.

The negative consequence of pursuing economic activity on the Sabbath is this: not only do we avoid giving God the fullness of our time and enjoying rest, but we also make others work on our behalf. This goes against the expressed purpose of Sabbath laid down by God in Holy Scripture! (Exodus 20) As God would have it, the Supreme Court in the United States actually declared Blue Laws constitutional because they recognize that Blue Laws offer a day of rest for laborers. Wow![18]

At another level, I believe that it is no coincidence that in many ways, our country was physically healthier during this time period as well. When people have time to rest from work, they can spend time with their families. Their bodies can rest and experience the healing of God. They can go and experience the presence of God in worship at church and at home.

But you may be saying in the back of your mind: "One whole day without spending money? I don't know how practical or realistic that is." Although the thought of refraining from economic activity on Sundays or any other one day of the week may seem radical in today's nonstop, 24/7 culture, it is biblical, it is of God, it is healing.

---

[18]   http://worldpopulationreview.com/states/bluelawsby-state/

Modeling Sabbath gives us, our families, our businesses and the communities we live in the opportunity to give workers a great gift: rest! So, over time, strive to do your cooking or buying in a way that for one day, you refrain from all economic activity with the world. Over time, avoid spending money at the mall or on electronic retail on Sundays or another day, unless it is a dire emergency. I know it's a stretch, but imagine how deeply you are blessing your neighbors!

The importance of modeling economic Sabbath makes me think about one year when I spent Thanksgiving with my parents in Georgia. Since my phone case had broken recently, I needed to get a new case from the local mall. I went on the day before Thanksgiving, thinking that employees would have at least the day of Thanksgiving off. But, in conversation with the staff person at the repair store, I learned something heartbreaking. Because many people wanted to get the best sales on Black Friday, many stores in the mall were going to be opening up on Thursday evening. This meant that this staff person would not be able to share in the Thanksgiving feast with her family and rest, because some people just could not wait to buy some new clothes or a new pair of shoes. This is one of the harmful consequences of greed in our society: When we do not curb our own desires through self-control, other people suffer because of our selfishness.

But here is the Good News: when we begin to live in the spirit of Jubilee, we can provide rest for our neighbors! We can burn brightly with the love of Christ that ushers our neighbors into the restorative, restful wholeness of God for all of their lives. We can stem the tide of greed and restore the fruit of the Spirit of generosity in our communities and in our world. We can show the world what the abundant life of God looks like.

What's more, God says clearly in Scripture, that there is a blessing in Sabbath: there is a blessing in resting and letting our neighbors rest! (Exodus 20:8-11) So let's model economic Sabbath together; you can do this; we can do this!

4. Advocating for Financial Empowerment of the Poor

A final way we can embrace Jubilee economics individually, in our homes and businesses is by advocating for financial empowerment and sustained generosity toward the poor. This can take place in several ways, such as:

- Encouraging the promotion of a living wage in your town or city

- Giving impoverished members of your church and/or community access to financial planning or stewardship teaching[19]
- Hosting a class in your family, church or community centered around debt-relief and financial stewardship
- Encouraging your local government to treat local immigrant workers with care and compassion. This is not a partisan idea, but a biblical command from the Lord: "When an alien resides with you in your land, you shall not oppress the alien...you shall love the alien as yourself." (Leviticus 19:33)
- If you or your church is the leader of a nonprofit or for-profit business, make sure that your employees are paid fairly and have good opportunities for career and vocational advancement.
- Connecting with local resources for small business start-ups and entrepreneurship. In this way, more companies can catch on fire with the love of Jesus in their practices and model Jubilee economics to a wider culture.[20] [21]

---

[19] Dave Ramsey's Financial Peace is a great first resource: https://www.daveramsey.com/fpu. I also recommend Moneywise Live on Moody Radio as another excellent resource.

[20] Some starter resources: https://www.entrepreneur.com/article/219967

[21] https://www.jpmorganchase.com/impact/people/advancing-black-pathways/advancingblackentrepreneurs/

Wonderful Person, no matter who you are or how many financial resources God has entrusted in your care, now is a moment to empower our neighbors through Jubilee economics. Like Moses, Jesus Christ and the followers of Jesus throughout the ages thunder powerfully, we can be the ones who say to the greedy, harmful powers of the age: in the name of Jesus Christ: "Let my People Go!"

God is waiting on us to bring this economic restoration into our communities and our land. Will you answer the call?

rice-chase-lounge

Heart Check Wrap-up

Key Points:

- Jubilee is God's gift for all people and creation: rest from labor and rest from harmful economic practices.
- God desires that all God's creation, the poor, and the exploited in society, experience rest and economic liberation.
- Empowering our neighbors through Jubilee principles involves four practices:
  o Embracing Kingdom abundance and generosity
  o Personal and corporate fasting from unjust labor practices and exploitive businesses
  o Modeling Sabbath by refraining from economic activity one day a week
  o Advocating for financial empowerment of the poor

Thoughts and Questions for Reflection:
- Share a time when you experienced Sabbath rest on a Sunday or another day of the week. How did it feel resting and allowing other people to rest from working on your behalf? If you have not, try it soon!
- How might you use this time of rest to empower and uplift your neighbors in need around you?
- What are some businesses you, your family, and/or your local Christian community could support in your community that model Jubilee rest for the poor?
- How might God be positioning you to practice empowering impoverished people in your Church or community?

Prayer: Dear Holy and Gracious God, thank you that you made all of creation to rest, including me. Forgive me for moments when my greed and hungers have brought harm to my neighbors. Give me faith and courage in you to practice Jubilee principles daily. Show me how to empower my neighbors in need through Jubilee rest and restoration so all people might worship You and enjoy your rest. In Jesus Christ's name. Amen.

CHAPTER 12

One Amazing Party: Witnessing to Our Neighbors

Wonderful Person, have you ever been to a really fun party? If so, were you the life of that party? (Smile.) In my life, God has blessed me to be a part of some great parties: birthday parties, ordination parties, wedding parties and more! There's something really exciting about a great party: everyone there is celebrating that something wonderful is taking place. There's music, fun, dance, games and usually a great feast of food!

Now imagine that great party you went to again. If you had such great fun there, if you could, would you invite someone to join you at the next party?

In the spiritual sense, this is what the practice of witnessing is, Wonderful Person. When we accept our invitation to join Jesus at the party of the Kingdom of God, the unlimited happiness of His love burning brightly in us and among us in other followers of Jesus starts its own party. Witnessing is inviting others into the great party of the love of Jesus! It is what happens when we joyfully share the Good News of how Jesus's love, excitement and divine direction have set our hearts and lives on fire and helped us change the world!

Scripture helps us understand in the Gospel of Luke. When Jesus is invited over to someone's house after worship (I wonder what they cooked!), He describes the Kingdom of God as a joyful party in the parable of the wedding banquet in Luke 14:15-24. In this timeless story, a person with great generosity threw a huge party. He invited his workers to go and invite many people to the party. Unfortunately, many people said no on their personal or electronic RSVP. Getting angry at this, the party host told his workers to go into the streets, calling in the poor, the crippled, lame and blind to the party. After they had done so, they told the man: "What you have ordered has been done and there is still room." Because of the man's great desire for all to feast, he sends them back out, calling people from all places to come in!

Like the man who longs for all people to come to his banquet, so Jesus longs for all of us and all people from the entire human family to feast at the party of His holy love. This is one amazing party!

If we are honest, it doesn't take a long look around our world to see why Jesus's party has so much appeal, excitement and life in it. In the midst of a world torn apart by sin, brokenness, greed, inequality and prejudice, Jesus's party embodied in His Church is a foretaste of the Kingdom of heaven! At Jesus's party, everyone is welcome, no matter their gender, age, ethnicity, ability level, or any other human classification! At Jesus's party, everyone who receives His invitation comes into abundant life, eternal life, a rich life of love of God, neighbor, self and divine purpose in this life!

Once our hearts burn with the excitement and love of Jesus Christ, we should be joyful people. Our joy is the warm, spiritually life-giving fire that draws in all people to Christ through us: individually, in our families, our Christian communities, our communities and throughout the entire Church around the globe.

Luke helps us understand even further in Holy Scripture through the Acts of the Apostles.

In Acts 1, Jesus is about to ascend after His Resurrection. After 40 days of spending time with the disciples, His time of preparation to get them ready for their life's mission is coming to an end. But He speaks of a promise to them: "You shall receive power when the Holy Spirit has come upon you, and you will be my witnesses in Jerusalem, in Judea, Samaria and to the ends of the earth." (Acts 1:8)

10 days later, Jesus's party gets started on the Day of Pentecost. The Bible says on the Day of Pentecost, all of the 120 disciples were gathered in one place in the Upper

Room. (Acts 2:1) Suddenly, there came a sound as of the rushing of a violent wind, and it filled the entire house where they were sitting.

The joy that the disciples felt about Jesus's resurrection was now beginning to spread like a holy wildfire. As the Holy Spirit fell with divided tongues, all of them were filled with the Holy Spirit and they began to speak in other languages. Luke records that the crowds gathered for the Pentecost harvest festival in Jerusalem could now hear God's deeds of power in their own languages. Wow!

Wonderful Person, this is the practice of witnessing which we are still invited into so many years later. It is sharing with our neighbors, our families, and others the Good News of Jesus Christ based on our own happy experience of Jesus's love, divine direction and powerful presence in our lives.

Our witness begins with our life and personal experience with Jesus. So what joy, what eternal happiness has Christ brought into your life? How have you experienced His resurrection hope and life? How has He healed you? That's the heart of your witness!

It makes me think about my first Sunday as a pastor in Atlanta, GA several years ago. In my own joy, I shared the Good News of the love of Jesus Christ during the sermon. I shared passionately about the authenticity of my own experience of Jesus Christ. After the sermon, I opened the doors of the church. In response, two men, children of

God who had committed crimes in their past, gave their lives to Jesus Christ and joined the Church that day. They became committed followers of Jesus because His love was now burning in their hearts!

It makes me think about a food pantry ministry at another church I served. This ministry was a great draw for bringing new people into our church. It became the door for bringing one woman into a deeper experience of the amazing, loving grace of Jesus Christ. She wrote me a letter after her first experience at the pantry and said: "I have grown up in church...but I have never experienced the love of Jesus Christ like this in my entire life."

So Wonderful Person, witnessing isn't about throwing a Bible at someone. Instead, people are looking to see Jesus in us! When the love and grace of Jesus Christ burns brightly in our hearts and in our lives, the Holy Spirit will bring forth the Gospel in all we do, in how we speak and how we live.

So again, what has Jesus done in your life? That is the source of your witness — a testimony that no one can take away! The world needs your witness of Jesus Christ. Like the first apostles, God has sent you and I to be evangelists, witnesses of the Good News for such a time as this!

Let's invite everyone we know to this amazing party, the party of the kingdom of God! When we do, people of all nations, tribes and tongues can come to know Jesus as Lord, Savior, and Messiah! What a great party this will be!

Heart Check Wrap-up

Key Points:

- The practice of witnessing is about sharing our testimony: inviting all people to the amazing party of Jesus's love by sharing our story of His love in our lives.
- Our witness begins with our walk as followers of Jesus: people should see Jesus reflected in our lives. Then we can invite them into a Christlike experience: an encounter with Christ in worship, prayer, a small group, etc.

Thoughts and Questions for Reflection:

- Has this book been your first introduction to who Jesus is? If so, how would you describe your meeting Him so far?
- If you are already in a relationship with Jesus, when did that relationship first begin? Who was responsible for nurturing you in His love?

- Name one or two persons in your friend group or
  community that do not have a relationship with
  God in Jesus Christ. How can you invite them into
  a Christlike experience in your life or your church?

Prayer: Gracious and Loving God, thank you for the joy
of the Gospel. Thank you for sending your Son to save
me and save all of humanity from our sins and give us the
gift of eternal life in this life and the life to come. Give me
courage to share the joy of Jesus's love and life that I've
found with those around me. Show me who in my life
needs to come into a new relationship with you. All these
things I pray in the name of Jesus Christ, my Lord and
Messiah. Amen.

SECTION IV

Epilogue

CHAPTER 13

The Sending: Hearts Strangely Warmed For All Generations

Over the years, I have learned something about fires: when a fire is lit and it is burning brightly, it is hard to put out. It is the same in the spiritual realm as well.

I remember when the spiritual fire of my calling was lit as a teenager, and my heart has burned with a passion for Jesus Christ since that moment. One moment during the season of first answering my calling stands out for a lifetime.

When I was sixteen or seventeen years of age, I remember singing a song at my teenage church, Crestwood UMC. It was a song sung by Christian musician John Michael Talbot. The song, "Here I am Lord", echoes an important conversation between the participant and God.

The verses of the song are three invitations from God to the believer, to the church…and at the closing stanza of each verse, the words share: "Whom shall I send" and the response is this from the chorus:

> "Here I am Lord, is it I Lord?
> I have heard you calling in the night! I will go
> Lord, if you lead me, I will hold your people in
> my heart.[22]"

Wonderful Person, I believe that the same clarion call from God is ringing out to each of us this day, to all who would live with hearts set on fire with the incredible, life-changing love, excitement, passion and purpose of Jesus Christ.

Just as the disciples were sent forth by Jesus after their encounter with the risen Christ, so Jesus is yearning to send us as well. He yearns to send us both as individuals and as groups of Jesus followers.

He longs to send us as a movement of people from every nation, tribe, and tongue under heaven. (Revelation 7:9) He longs to send us so that we might set our families, our communities, our institutions and our world on fire with the love we have been loved with, the love of Jesus that has welcomed us home into His arms.

So if your heart has been set on fire with Christ's love, let's go! If His love is overflowing like a holy wildfire in

---

[22]   https://www.youtube.com/watch?v=gZK-5v9gMTI

your life through these timeless values of God's grace and these timeless practices of loving your neighbor, let's go!

Jesus gave a fresh commission to the disciples at the end of His time in the earth that helps us to understand in Scripture. Matthew records in the Gospel of Matthew 28:20 that this was the Great Commission, a graduation speech for the disciples. Jesus gave to them and to us a great mission that has changed and always will change the world: "Go and make disciples of all nations, baptizing them in the name of the Father and the Son and of the Holy Spirit, teaching them to do everything I have commanded you." God is calling you, have you answered your call? Jesus Christ is calling you, have you responded, Wonderful Person?

I imagine that like some of us, the first disciples might not have felt so great in their own abilities upon hearing this Great Commission. They might have wondered about their capacity for setting the world on fire for Christ and His love. Thanks be to God that Jesus follows the Great Commission with a Great Promise! Jesus says: "And remember, I will be with you always, even to the end of the age!" (Matthew 28:20)

Wonderful Person, God is calling us in Christ Jesus: go and make disciples! Go set the world on fire with the love of Jesus Christ! Go establish the reign of God in every family, every nation, among every tribe where you are!

I'm going to go, how about you?

Let's go set more hearts on fire! In the name of the Father, Son and Holy Spirit. Amen.

Book References

1. Alexander, Michelle. The New Jim Crow: Mass Incarceration in an Age of Colorblindness. New York: The New Press, 2012.
2. Augustine of Hippo. Confessions. University of California: Collier: 1909.
3. Deymaz, Mark. Building a Healthy Multi-Ethnic Church. San Francisco: John Wiley & Sons, Inc, 2007.
4. Deymaz, Mark and Okuwobi, Oneya Fennell. Multi-Ethnic Conversations: an eight-week journey toward unity in your church. Indianapolis: Wesleyan Publishing House, 2016.
5. The Division of Christian Education of the National Council of the Churches of Christ in the United States of America. The New Revised Standard Version Bible. 1989.
6. King, James. Christlike Love Unit, 2013.
7. Outler, Albert C. and Heizenrater, Richard P. John Wesley's Sermons: An Anthology. Abingdon Press, Nashville, 1991.

8. The United Methodist Publishing House. The United Methodist Hymnal: Book of United Methodist Worship. Nashville, 1989.

The Hearts On Fire Prayer

Dear God,
Thank you for the unconditional love, divine direction,
purpose and exciting life you have for me in Jesus
I offer you my heart to be set on fire with
Your love today
As you set my heart on fire, help me spread the fire
of your love by loving my neighbors as I love myself
wherever I am
So that all may live with hearts on fire all
around the world
In Jesus Christ's name I pray. Amen.

CPSIA information can be obtained
at www.ICGtesting.com
Printed in the USA
LVHW081737250721
693540LV00008B/16